Endorsements

Cheryl has provided a powerful read of practical theology in *Securely Held*. What do we do when our theology doesn't match our reality and we need to move our destructive doubts and emotions into healthy habits rooted in truth? *Securely Held* takes us by the hand and walks us toward the life God promised. For the woman who wants more from her relationship with God, come and be held in His everlasting arms.

—**Erica Wiggenhorn,** *international speaker and author*
of An Unexpected Revival: Experiencing God's Goodness
Through Disappointment and Doubt, an eight-week study
on the power of the Holy Spirit through the prophecies of Ezekiel.

Securely Held feels like the culmination of an awe-inspiring journey. I first met Cheryl over ten years ago—an immensely gifted woman who, at the time, hadn't fully developed her true voice. As a friend, I was privileged to watch an incredible transformation unfold as she dove into the intricate tangles of self-doubt and insecurities that held her back.

Through a profound revelation of God's unwavering love, Cheryl now fully embraces her calling. And on the days my people-pleasing, approval-seeking tendencies override my common sense, I'm so grateful for that. She knows (and teaches) the truth: genuine validation and steadfast security flow solely from God.

In *Securely Held*, Cheryl guides us into the very essence of God's heart and helps us anchor our lives there. As we learn to embrace and rest in His love, we unearth a joy and strength that helps us confidently walk in our purpose.

—*Jo Ann Fore, personal growth mentor and author of When a Woman Finds Her Voice: Overcoming Life's Hurts & Using Your Story to Make a Difference*

Securely Held is a poignant journey that answers the universal question of who we are by reminding us that all depends on who we know and belong to. Through the personal testimony of others and various Bible characters, we learn better why this must be our approach in order to find ourselves "securely held." We *can* trust the everlasting arms of our Father, because He has proved himself faithful throughout history and in the lives of our contemporaries. Highly relatable and honest—I give this book a big thumbs-up.

—*Diana Lee Flegal, YouTuber (Reality Coaching for Writers), Freelance Editor, and Writing Coach*

A fresh start for the weary heart! Cheryl Lutz understands the heart of those who want to be unseen, to simply blend in with the crowd. Through biblical stories and her experience, she shares the promise of God's presence and the reasons to be boldly seen and used by Him. *Securely Held* holds the key to transforming the mind, therefore setting the prisoners free to experience victory.

—*Tammy Whitehurst,* leader at the Christian Communicators Conference in chapter 1, TammyWhitehurst.com

We often feel we're not enough—even for those who love us. We also often feel we have to perform to a certain level so as to be worthy of that love. *Securely Held* assures us that God loves us and that we are worthy of that love. I highly recommend this book!

—*Janet Holm McHenry,* speaker and author of twenty-five books, including the bestselling *PrayerWalk*

Need some inspiration and courage to break free from striving for validation? Look no further than Cheryl Lutz's uplifting book! With enlightening storytelling, biblical truths, and plenty of wisdom from personal experience, it will help you find true freedom from approval seeking. Get ready for an empowered journey toward living a truly fulfilling life with a deeper understanding of your heavenly Father's love for you.

—*Mary R Snyder,* speaker coach and podcast host of *Take the Stage*

Securely Held

Securely Held

Finding Significance and Security in the Shelter of God's Embrace

Cheryl Pelton Lutz

Foreword by Dr. Charley L. Chase

Published by Redemption Press, PO Box 427, Enumclaw, WA 98022.

Toll-Free (844) 2REDEEM (273-3336)

Redemption Press is honored to present this title in partnership with the author. The views expressed or implied in this work are those of the author. Redemption Press provides our imprint seal representing design excellence, creative content, and high-quality production.

Disclaimer: Although the stories in this book are factual, certain names and identifying information have been altered to safeguard the privacy of those involved. Additionally, the narrative may contain some creative liberties taken by the author in order to effectively tell the story.

ISBN 13: 978-1-64645-659-8
ISBN eBook: 978-1-64645-661-1
Library of Congress Catalog Card Number: 2023913554

Cheryl

A doe in the forest—always on guard
So fragile, so lithe—trying so hard
Not showing the fears—the caring inside
Emotions within—soon to rise like the tide.
A flower blooming, the beauty so fresh
So sweet, so special—beginning to mesh
Looking for answers—not quite understanding
So many things of life demanding.
A child—a woman—then child again
Part of the puzzle—the master plan
Cheryl—sweet Cheryl—sixteen so soon
A good life awaits you—eat from its spoon.

—Glenda Brown Pelton

I so look forward to our eternal reunion.

Contents

Foreword   xiii

Acknowledgments   xv

Section One Finding Our Identity in God's Embrace

Chapter One   Who Am I?   19

Chapter Two   Am I Safe in This Relationship?   33

Chapter Three   Will I Ever Find Acceptance?   47

Chapter Four   Where Do I Find Deliverance?   61

Section Two Finding our Significance in God's Embrace

Chapter Five   Why Do I Still Feel Shame?   77

Chapter Six   Does God See Me?   91

Chapter Seven   How Do I Release My Adult Children?   105

Chapter Eight   Where Is My Significance Found?   119

Section Three Finding Rest in God's Embrace

Chapter Nine   Why Am I So Tired?   137

Chapter Ten   Why Can't I Ask for Help?   151

Chapter Eleven   Why Am I So Anxious?   163

Chapter Twelve   Where Do I Find Healing and Rest?   175

Epilogue   193

A Note from Cheryl's Husband   197

About the Author   201

Notes   203

Recommended Resources for Responding to Abuse   209

Bibliography of Books and Websites for Story Contributors   213

Foreword

In 1980, country music artist Johnny Lee's "Looking for Love in All the Wrong Places" spread its lyrical wings and soared to the top of the charts. True to its storytelling genre, the song chronicles a modern knight's quest for the lady of his dreams. After a search in vain, bleak loneliness morphs into blissful love as he finally meets the one who contents him.

Cheryl Lutz's *Securely Held: Finding Significance and Security in the Shelter of God's Embrace* sings the spiritual version of a similar, yet far more important, quest no small number of women find themselves on. The love they're seeking goes beyond the realm of marriage and romantic relationships. Instead, these struggling, stifled, suffering women are seeking a love that transcends a husband's love (and every other earthly love), as surely as the taste of honey surpasses the mere description of its sweetness. Their quest is for a love that seizes their being as fully as joy captures a child on Christmas morning. For a love that meets the gnawing craving for significance: *I am indescribably important to someone.* For a love that meets the searing yearning for security: *I have someone taking care of me who's big enough for the job.* And for a love that lays an unshakable foundation for serenity: *I belong to someone who frees me from the corrosive relational rust of a people-pleasing, fearful, shame-governed lifestyle.*

Alas, like Lee's searcher in the song, it's easy to look for love in all the wrong places. In biblical terms, they try to quench their raging thirst for security, significance, and serenity at broken cisterns that hold no water. Because Cheryl has been on this quest and knows these cisterns are drought empty, she understands other women and their similar quest.

Wonderfully, however, Cheryl hasn't only been to the broken cisterns. Through the finished work of Christ, she's also been to the living spring called the heavenly Father's embrace. Drinking deeply and daily at this satisfying spring, she is able to quench her thirst for that love that alone fulfills a woman's (and man's) deepest longing to be securely held.

Evangelism has been rightly described as one beggar telling another beggar where to find bread. This book can rightly be described as one securely held woman telling other women how they, too, can become securely held. And oh, how she shares her message! Her wise counsel is Scripture-soaked; raw with a realism that echoes the Psalms; abundant in application that's pointed, practical, and profitable; effervescent with the eloquence of conviction generated by personal experience; and all wrapped in gentle prose that makes Mr. Rogers seem as ornery as the prodigal's older brother.

I have for many years been encouraging this godly, gifted, gracious lady to find her voice and share it with us. I'm happy to say she has found it. I hear it in this book. I hope you'll read it and hear it too. You will find that in the shelter of your heavenly Father's embrace you are securely held.

—*Dr. Charley L. Chase,*
pastor of Community Church, Griffin, Georgia,
and author of Good, Good Father and
Grace-Focused Optimism

Acknowledgments

To my husband, Alan, you have loved me unconditionally since our first date in 1988. You are my greatest earthly blessing. Thank you for loving me so well and always making me feel cherished.

To our four adult children: Hannah, Daniel, Abigail, and Joseph. You are my greatest earthly treasures. Thank you for loving me despite my parenting failures. My prayer for each of you is that you will look to the one who will never fail you—the Lord Jesus Christ.

To my first two writing coaches, Janet McHenry and Sue Fairchild. Janet, you believed in my project before I did, and your teaching on form and structure gave me the framework for this book. Sue, you have become a dear friend, and your editing expertise has been invaluable!

To our best friends, Jeff and Holly Duncan. Thank you for walking beside Alan and me in the hard and in the happy. We love you!

To Tammy Whitehurst and Lori Boruff. The Christian Communicator's Conference in 2020 both wrecked me and shaped me. I am grateful to you both for your exceptional guidance and invaluable feedback, which have contributed significantly to my development as a Christian communicator.

To my speaking coach extraordinaire, Mary R. Snyder. Your Activate course took my speaking ministry to the next level. You are loved and appreciated!

To my praying partners, Christine, Missy, and Stacy. I am so grateful for each of you—your faithful prayers kept me moving forward. To all my beloved CCC Sistas, you know who you are, and especially Mel. Thank you for praying and talking me out of packing my suitcase and leaving the conference! Last, I thank Melony, Shelly, Natasha, Christina, Missy E, Judy, Missy L, Phylis, Michelle, and Christine, for bravely sharing their personal stories.

Finding Our Identity in God's Embrace

Chapter One

Who Am I?

Moses said to God, "Who am I that I should go to
Pharaoh and bring the children of Israel
out of Egypt?"

EXODUS 3:11

I reminded myself to breathe and tried to swallow as I felt my throat beginning to constrict and my tongue sticking to the roof of my mouth. I sat in Miss Greg's sixth-grade class, silently pleading, *Please don't call my name today!* It was the loathsome oral report day, and I was afraid to look up and risk meeting the teacher's gaze. So I kept my eyes fixed on the groove engraved across my desk. I remember the comforting sensation of rubbing my finger on the smooth surface carved there to support my pencil from rolling away. But suddenly my finger froze, just like the rest of my body, when I heard the word I dreaded hearing: *Cheryl.*

I didn't want to be known or called by name. I just wanted to be invisible.

Have you ever wished to remain unseen? When you were in middle school, did you dread the teacher calling your name to answer a homework question or present something to the class? Or have you ever felt so self-conscious that you wished for an invisibility cloak to drape over you until you were ready to face your fears? This immobilizing insecurity stems from a lack of understanding of who we are. Using our voices to speak, share, and present takes confidence. But we have no self-assurance if we don't know who we are.

Back in that sixth-grade classroom, I desperately wanted to conjure up self-confidence, but I didn't know who I was. And unfortunately, there was no robe available to disguise my presence. Nor did I have Frodo's ring from *The Hobbit* to slip on my finger so I could make my escape unseen. Instead, I arose from my desk and sensed the heat rising from the tip of my toes to the top of my head. Then, with my heart pounding and knees shaking and staring at the pencil shavings littering the linoleum squares, I made my way to the front of the classroom. As I tried to slow my rapid breathing, the smell of sweaty boys fresh from baseball practice filled my nostrils. When I finally opened my mouth to read my report, I couldn't find my voice. With eyes stinging and salty tears running down my cheeks, I was excused by the teacher to go to the restroom to wash my face. I thought I would suffocate in that bathroom as deep shame and embarrassment engulfed me. I desperately wanted to cry out, "Beam me up, Scotty," as I had heard so many times on *Star Trek*, and blast off into space with my preteen crush, Captain Kirk. Alas, the *Starship Enterprise* never arrived!

In her book *When a Woman Finds Her Voice: Overcoming Life's Hurts and Using Your Story to Make a Difference*, my friend and author Jo Ann Fore writes: "For the soul-wounded woman. Your healed voice is my favorite sound. Your hurts, they walk right into our hearts; but your story of healing—that can change lives. Never be afraid to find and use your voice."[1]

Jo Ann says unresolved wounds can leave us silent or afraid to be ourselves, but hope and healing can be our portion if we are willing to do the soul work that brings lasting hope. Finding our voice and our God-given identity takes time and energy to address the reasons we lost our individuality in the first place.

Perhaps you can relate to that shy little girl in middle school desperately searching for her identity. Or maybe you didn't shake like a leaf and turn the color of Bob the Tomato as I did, but have you ever felt suffocated by fear and insecurity? Have you ever been so intimidated that you remained silent rather than risking making your voice heard?

Making our voices heard relates to how we express ourselves. Not receiving enough encouragement and positive affirmations in our formative years can stifle creative expression. Sometimes unresolved trauma can make us believe our voice doesn't matter. Or maybe it isn't safe to express our individuality. This leads to paralyzing shyness and social anxiety.

Some of us experienced being securely held by our earthly fathers, but many do not share that blessing. Some women are securely held by our earthly husbands, yet some have not experienced comforting and protective love. But the Bible shows us that if we have a relationship with Jesus, we are securely held by our heavenly Father, no matter what our earthly relationships look like! In each chapter of *Securely Held*, we will examine a riveting Bible story that demonstrates someone who discovers their voice and identity. As these biblical figures gain an understanding of who God is, we will see them realize who they are.

The Journey to Discovering Who We Are Begins with God's Word

Did you know the prophet Moses struggled to find his voice? In Exodus 3:1–15, the angel of the Lord appeared to Moses amid a flaming bush and called him to return to his people and rescue them from Pharaoh in Egypt. I like to believe that if God spoke to me in such a miraculous way and gave me specific instructions regarding the who, what, when, where, and how part of my calling, the way He did for Moses, I would run and pack my bags with fury and excitement to answer the call! However, Moses answered God with a question, which would likely have also been my response. Moses asked, "Who am I that I should go to Pharaoh and bring the children of Israel out of Egypt?" (Exodus 3:11). We know from Moses's question that he felt inadequate for the task and fearful of the assignment. *Who am I?* At the core of his question is insecurity regarding his identity and ability.

After being called to fulfill a significant task, have you ever asked, *Who am I?* Perhaps, instead of wondering who you are, you have a running list of who you aren't. Not smart enough, not educated enough, not pretty enough, not small enough, tall enough, eloquent enough, etc.

Who am I? To answer Moses's question, let's look at his upbringing. Scripture tells us in Exodus 1 that Moses was born during a horrific genocide. Although the previous ruler welcomed the Israelites into the land, Pharaoh was intimidated by their strength and massive population. In order to decrease their population, Pharaoh instructed that all newborn male Israelites be killed.

But in Exodus 2, a unique Hebrew child is birthed onto the scene. Moses was born to Amram (from the house of Levi) and Jochebed.

Who Am I?

Scripture says his mother recognized that he was a "fine child," and she kept him hidden for three months. Of course, I must chuckle as I think, *What mother doesn't believe her baby boy is a fine child?* Yet his parents must have perceived something unusually special about him. Perhaps they saw that he might be the one to bring deliverance to their people. Theologian John Calvin said, "There was some mark, as it were, of future excellency imprinted on the child, which gave promise of something extraordinary."[2]

Clearly, Calvin suggests that Moses's parents recognized a calling on the child's life and knew they were to keep him alive so he could fulfill an essential assignment in the future. God reveals that their perceptions were accurate. A glimpse of the child's uniqueness is also found in Acts 7:20, which says Moses was "beautiful in God's sight." We know that this beauty encompassed more than outward appearance. We learn about God's determination of beauty in 1 Samuel 16 when God calls David to replace Saul as king of Israel. Samuel looked at David's older brothers' tall, muscular statures, believing God would choose one of them to be king. But God said to Samuel, "For the Lord sees not as man sees: man looks on the outward appearance, but the Lord looks on the heart" (1 Samuel 16:7). God does not choose those for service based on outward beauty. Instead, unlike man, God makes His judgments based on the character of the heart.

God's calling on Moses's life is demonstrated after his parents hide him in a basket and place it by the river. Baby Moses is found and then adopted by the daughter of the very Pharaoh that called for his death—an extraordinary situation demonstrating that Moses was beloved of the Lord and set apart for an exceptional calling. Pharaoh's daughter raised Moses as her son, and "he was instructed in all the wisdom of the Egyptians, and he was mighty in his words and deeds" (Acts 7:22).

Moses had reason to be grateful for God's divine intervention and the preservation of his life. His privileged Egyptian education and the luxuries of palace living were further reasons for gratitude. Yet Moses's adoption and lifestyle were unconventional for a biological Hebrew, likely causing turmoil and confusion within him. Perhaps he wrestled with feelings of guilt because of the oppression his adoptive grandfather inflicted on his Hebrew race. He also likely struggled with finding where he fit in amid these conflicting environments.

Yet since the fall of humanity in the garden of Eden, all families have been dysfunctional, whether biological or adoptive. A pastor friend of ours used to say, "It is only by God's grace that anything good could come out of sinners raising sinners!" Despite life's heartaches and dysfunction, however, we can be grateful for God's hand in preserving our life and calling … like Moses.

In Acts 7, Moses is forty years old and still living as Pharaoh's grandson in the palace. But one day, he decides to go and visit the children of Israel. When he sees an Israelite being mistreated, he avenges the man by killing the Egyptian who was oppressing him. The next day, instead of his people appreciating him, when Moses tells them they should not be quarreling among themselves, one man's indignant response is "Who made you a ruler and a judge over us? Do you want to kill me as you killed the Egyptian yesterday?" (Acts 7:27–28). Yikes! His fellow Hebrews respond quite differently than he expected.

Have you ever sacrificed your position or reputation to defend someone, only to have them turn on you? It's soul-crushing. Your probable first response—to vow never to do that good deed again. But keep your eyes on God and not on man and realize the reason for doing the right thing is not about receiving the outcome but about bringing God glory. I know, it's much easier said than done. I know the pain of betrayal well, but healing is a process that takes place over time as you press into Him. As you work through the pain, God provides the boldness to step out in faith and trust again.

Not only does Moses have to handle the scorn directed at him, but he also realizes there were witnesses to the murder of the Egyptian and that Pharaoh is furious. He discerns that his life is now in danger, so he leaves his privilege and position in Egypt to flee to the land of Midian to avoid Pharaoh's wrath. In Midian, he meets a priest named Jethro, marries one of his daughters, and becomes a shepherd.

So who was Moses? As we look at his upbringing and life experiences, it's easy to see why he would have been confused about his identity. When his adoption was jeopardized because he had murdered an Egyptian, was he no longer the son of Pharaoh's daughter? Was he back to being an Israelite and the son of a couple from the house of Levi? Or did living as a shepherd in Midian make him a Midianite shepherd?

Have you ever wrestled with understanding your identity because of a confusing or traumatic past? Has being afraid of getting burned ever kept you trapped in your comfort zone? Have you ever felt like a timid turtle, afraid to come out of your shell? Perhaps after God spoke to Moses and called him to return to Egypt and rescue his people, he thought, *Been there, done that. It didn't work the first time I tried to help them, so why try again?* Furthermore, after his last attempt, the Hebrews responded with "Who are you?" and the Egyptians put a bounty on his head! No, thank you. Moses was happy with his new family, leading a quiet life as a shepherd. But God was showing Moses it was time to step out of his comfort zone and fulfill the calling placed on his life as an infant.

Moses asked God, "Who am I that I should go to the children of Israel?" Listen to God's answer: "But I will be with you, and this shall be the sign for you that I have sent you: when you have brought the people out of Egypt, you shall serve God on this mountain" (Exodus 3:12). God promises Moses His presence. Moses will not be left abandoned, struggling to complete the assignment independently. The same is true for us, dear reader. God doesn't call us and then watch from a distance to see if we mess up. Instead, He fills us with His Spirit, and His presence goes before us, beside us, and behind us.

Who Is God?

Moses's second question, however, is a much more vital one. In Exodus 3:13, he asks, "If I come to the people of Israel and say to them, 'The God of your fathers has sent me to you,' and they ask me, 'What is his name?' what shall I say to them?" God reveals His magnificence in His answer to Moses's question, saying, "I Am WHO I Am." And he said, "Say this to the people of Israel: 'I Am has sent me to you'" (Exodus 3:14).

Who is God? Moses already knew that God had revealed Himself as the God of their fathers, the God of Abraham, Isaac, and Jacob. But in the above verse, Moses asks God for His personal name. In that culture, names had significant meaning. Pastor and author John Piper said, "In Scripture, a person's name often signifies his character or ability, or mission—especially when the name is given by God."[3] I believe Piper is saying we see God's magnificent character and eternal power and glory displayed through His personal name—and that God's intimate name reveals His mission to give us a way to know Him personally.

Who Am I?

Who is God? is the question we should all start with when questioning who we are or when wondering if we are equipped for an assignment. When we begin to grasp a more accurate picture of who God is, we begin to understand who we are.

The Sustainer of the universe is our personal and tender shepherd, and He cares about every aspect of our lives. Ephesians 2:10 assures us of this truth: "For we are his workmanship, created in Christ Jesus for good works, which God prepared beforehand, that we should walk in them." Workmanship is artistry done with the hands. We are each uniquely crafted by the very hands of the master artist. We have been recreated in Christ for good works. We don't have to invent His will for our lives or strive for His approval. Instead, like Moses, we can confidently walk in the good works He has already laid out for us.

Discovering Hope and Healing

As I think back to my lack of confidence to speak in front of the class in middle school, I didn't know who I was because I didn't understand who God was (and is) as my Father: the great I Am, revealed to us through His Son. I am grateful He is repurposing my past and showing me who I am as His beloved daughter. Friend, He will do the same for you!

Fast-forward to 2020 when I attended the Christian Communicators Conference at the Billy Graham Center in North Carolina. Yes, the girl who couldn't even give an oral book report in middle school and had struggled with extreme shyness and social anxiety most of her adult life was at a conference to learn to be a Christian public speaker! This was a true testimony to God's healing power and divine call.

Before the event, one of the directors asked for three volunteers to present a devotion during our time together. As a pastor's wife who had taught Bible studies for almost thirty years at that point, I thought it would be safe for me to volunteer, and I was chosen to present a devotion on the first day of the conference. I was nervous speaking to a group of speakers but also encouraged by the privilege and felt my message was well-received and edified the ladies.

However, on the second day of the event, everything changed. One of the conference directors gave further instructions on the art of presenting. One of the things she mentioned several times was that we were *speakers, not readers*. I remembered that I had read parts of the devotion I had given, and my thoughts began to swirl. I was convinced she was speaking directly to me, and I was embarrassed that she had let me share the devotion the day before. Then, because I did not check my thoughts, they continued to spiral downward. Instead of trusting in the power of God's Word and Spirit, I made the devotion about me and my need for approval.

Suddenly, the Enemy of my soul began convincing me that everyone at the conference knew the leader was speaking directly to me regarding my poor delivery and that everyone there felt sorry for me. I was transported back to that sixth-grade classroom! That afternoon, I found myself hiding in my private room, lying on the bed, crying, and wanting to go home.

I was convinced that becoming a speaker was all a big mistake. Thankfully, after some rest and sustenance, a new friend I met at the conference talked me out of packing my suitcase. (It's amazing how a snack, a nap, and a sweet friend can bring perspective.) That evening, I told the story of my afternoon meltdown to one of the leaders. I also shared with her about what happened in sixth grade. She looked into my eyes and said, "You're not that scared little girl anymore." That was another lightbulb moment for me. You see, healing comes in layers and is a lifelong journey. And the Enemy of our souls is relentless in hitting us when we're weak—especially in the areas in which we've fought so hard for victory. That is why we all need a community of like-minded sisters we can encourage and who can, likewise, encourage us.

So grab a notebook, pen, and Bible, and let's discover together:

- Release from gaining security and validation through approval-seeking
- Clarity in your understanding of your heavenly Father's complete affirmation of you
- Renewed strength and purpose to share your story with others
- A rediscovery of the joy lacking in your work and ministry
- The confidence needed to walk in the good works God provides for you
- Liberation from fear of rejection
- The true meaning of loving God and others

A Prayer for His Beloved

Dear heavenly Father, I cry out to You, the great I AM. The one who brings out the starry host one by one and calls forth each of them by name. And by Your great power and mighty strength, not one of them is missing (Isaiah 40:26).

Father, You know my fears, and You know my hurts. Father, as You called out, "Moses, Moses" from that burning bush, I pray I will hear clearly as You call me by name. Father, as You named the stars and called them to fulfill Your good purpose, how much more have You named and called me, Your blood-bought daughter! May I step into my calling with confidence.

Lord, You who are enthroned on high from everlasting to everlasting, the one whose name is established forever, You are the King of Kings and Lord of Lords. Yet through the blood of Jesus, I can call You Abba, Father. Please help me understand who I am because of who You are.

Father, you promised Moses Your presence to go with him into Egypt, and may I know that promise is for me as well. I can go without fear wherever You call me because You will never leave me or forsake me along the way. And because of the precious name of Jesus, may I find rest in the shelter of Your embrace. In the name of Jesus, amen.

Questions for Reflection

Read Exodus 3:1–15.

1. Describe a time when you struggled to find your voice.
2. What was Moses's response when God instructed him to bring His children out of Egypt? (Exodus 3:11)
3. Why do you think Moses responded in that way?
4. What did God promise Moses in Exodus 3:12?
5. What did God tell Moses to say if the children of Israel asked the name of the one who had sent him? (Exodus 3:14, 15)

6. How does having a more profound comprehension of who God is, affect your understanding of who you are?
7. Think of a time when you didn't feel equipped for something you were called to do.
8. What emotions did you experience? Why do you think you reacted in that way?

Chapter Two

Am I Safe in This Relationship?

*It is better to take refuge in the Lord
than to trust in man.*

PSALM 118:8

He was driving me to work so he could use my car because his car was broken down again. I hadn't had my fire-engine-red Ford Mustang long, but I had saved up gift money from my recent high school graduation to make the down payment. It was a hot afternoon in Corpus Christi, Texas, and I was grateful to have the AC cranked, since my last car, a green Volkswagen Beetle, hadn't had air-conditioning. As the countdown of the top eighties hits blared on the radio, I thought about how nice it was not to have to arrive at work anymore with my back drenched in sweat.

The vibe in the car was disrupted, however, when Greg and I started arguing. As we pulled up to a red light, his anger about something I said hit a fever pitch, and he suddenly grabbed me by the back of my long brown ponytail and yanked it so hard my head snapped against the back of the headrest. In shock and embarrassment, I glanced over at the car beside us just in time to see the astonished look on the face of the man driving. Then the light turned green, and we drove forward as if nothing had happened. Greg would downplay the incident like always, and I would internalize feelings of blame and shame.

The first three years of our relationship had been a tumultuous time, and his talk about getting a college degree or going to a trade school had yet to materialize even though he was twenty-one. At eighteen, I now wanted to make plans of my own but was stuck in this abusive, dysfunctional relationship, due to my own lack of identity. I wanted to be loved and cared for, yet in the back of my mind, I thought an abusive relationship was better than being alone.

They say your high school years are the best days of your life, but those were the worst days of mine. I wish I had known then what I know now—identity insecurity breeds dysfunctional relationships that are unsafe spiritually, emotionally, and sometimes physically. Likewise, putting ultimate trust in others to satisfy our need for love and protection will always end in heartache. C. H. Spurgeon said, "The best of men are men at best."[4] The best people we know are still people who sin and make mistakes. God is the only one we can put our ultimate trust in. He is the only one who will never leave us or forsake us and will provide the safety we all crave.

During my first year at our local community college, a new and fun job opened for me working in a surf shop on Padre Island. I was no longer as isolated and began making new friends at school and work. Meeting other young men who had clear goals and a path forward in life emboldened me to finally break up with Greg for good.

He stalked me for months, however, and called my home nonstop, harassing me.

Then, a few months later, as I was driving to a friend's house, I noticed Greg following me in his truck. My stomach lurched as he came close to my bumper and then backed off time and time again. In my rearview mirror, I could see him clutching his wheel. When he motioned for me to pull over, I refused. This irritated him more, and he pulled up beside me and tried to force my car off the road. I gripped my own wheel harder and fought to stay on the road.

Eventually, I was able to pull ahead and drive in front of a delivery truck that Greg was stuck behind. This enabled me to beat him to my friend's house, where, with a pounding heart, I sprinted across her grass and made it into her house. He arrived soon after and began banging on her door. He left only when her mother threatened to call the police.

For months after this event, I would wake up to dreams about Greg finding me alone and killing me. Thankfully and to my surprise, however, the harassment abruptly ended. I always thought it was strange that after constant intimidation, he suddenly grew silent. As I write this chapter, however, I've come to the realization that my dad likely threatened him. I'll never know for sure since I never asked my dad, and he is now gone, but knowing how intimidating my dad could be, this makes sense.

What about you? Have you ever been in an unsafe relationship? Or have you looked to other people to meet needs that only God can meet? Is your identity wrapped up in earthly relationships that can never satisfy? Perhaps you never had a physically abusive husband or boyfriend, but have you ever been in an unhealthy friendship? What about a one-sided relationship where you are the only one who makes concessions? Perhaps it's always your responsibility to keep the peace and the other person happy. A relationship doesn't have to be physically abusive for it to be an unsafe space for your heart or spiritual growth.

Navigating Difficult Relationships

In a more recent season of my life, I participated in a fellowship group with some ladies, which started off as a fun and uplifting experience. However, due to the dynamics of various relationships and personalities in the group, I left in tears on a couple of occasions. Finally, my adult daughter said to me, "Mom, if you are leaving crying instead of laughing, it's not the right group for you anymore." I realized the wisdom of her words, and I had a final meeting with several of the ladies. I was confronted about some things, and I confronted some things. By God's grace, both sides extended apologies and forgiveness, but I knew my daughter was still right and that it wasn't the right group for me anymore. There was one woman in the fellowship who really struggled to like me. I did not need to continue attending the meetings, striving to gain her acceptance. I had to realize that though this woman loved me as a sister in Christ, she really didn't like me, and I needed to be okay with that.

News flash: there are people I love as fellow Christ-followers but don't particularly like or want to hang out with daily. We all have limited amounts of time, so we can choose friendships that are life giving to us and accept that a relationship doesn't have to be abusive or toxic for it to be unhealthy for our emotional or spiritual health.

Am I Safe in This Relationship?

A Discerning and Beautiful Woman and a Harsh and Badly Behaved Man

"Now the name of the man was Nabal, and the name of his wife Abigail. The woman was discerning and beautiful, but the man was harsh and badly behaved" (1 Samuel 25:3). In Samuel, we read about a harsh and foolish man named Nabal with a lovely and wise wife named Abigail. David and his men provide kindness and protection for the extremely wealthy Nabal and his men while they are shearing their sheep in the wilderness. In return, David requests that Nabal provide food for him and his men.

Sadly, the foolish Nabal's indignant response is "Who is David? Who is the son of Jesse? There are many servants these days who are breaking away from their masters. Shall I take my bread and my water and my meat that I have killed for my shearers and give it to men who come from I do not know where?" (1 Samuel 25:10–11). Upon hearing Nabal's words, David, in unbridled anger, instructs his men to strap on their swords, and he leads them out to murder Nabal and every male among him.

This is where the discerning and beautiful Abigail enters the scene. She learns of the actions and words of her worthless husband and how he repaid good with evil. Rather than cowering in fear and dread, Abigail immediately acts to save the lives of her people, without disclosing her plan to her foolish husband. She packs Nabal's men with gifts for David and his men, then goes to meet him and his army. When Abigail sees David, she quickly dismounts from her donkey, falls on her face before him, and says, "On me alone, my lord, be the guilt. Please let your servant speak in your ears, and hear the words of your servant. Let not my lord regard this worthless fellow,

Nabal, for as his name is, so is he. Nabal is his name, and folly is with him" (1 Samuel 25:24–25).

David accepts the gifts of provisions and heeds Abigail's advice to refrain from sinning by seeking his own vengeance against Nabal.

When Abigail returns home, she finds her drunk husband having a large feast in his house. She doesn't bother talking to him until the next morning after he has sobered up. She then relays to him what took place the day before, and he seemingly experiences a heart attack and dies ten days later.

God Provides for Abigail

David praised God when he learned of the wicked Nabal's death, then sent for Abigail. She willingly went with David's servants and became his wife.

Abigail's narrative is a beautiful example of the way to find deliverance from a toxic relationship and discover safety in God. Abigail knew who she was, and she was secure in her identity as God's daughter. She stayed humble before the Lord and did not allow her husband's insolence to keep her from acting wisely toward David. Even though we do not know how she ended up in that toxic marriage, we do know that in the culture in which she lived, she may not have had a choice. As she honored the Lord and chose wisdom in her dealings, God delivered her from the marriage to the evil Nabal and showed Himself to be her safe provider.

Accepting Safety

After I became less isolated, made new friends, and met some quality young men with plans for their future, I was able to break free of my own abusive relationship with my first boyfriend. It was soon after that I met and dated Mark, a navy pilot. I felt physically safe with Mark, but not emotionally, as I wrestled with insecurity, inferiority, and fear of abandonment. My fears were realized after we had been dating for a year; he got stationed in a different state and moved without making a commitment to me. Meanwhile on the heels of Mark's departure, we discovered my mother's breast cancer had metastasized. The doctor told my family she had only six months to live. It was a dark and lonely time for me, and I did not have Christian friends to help me navigate the grief. Instead of looking to God, I had put my trust in a man to provide the security and safety I craved—only to be let down again.

However, a bright light appeared when I met Alan Lutz. After being invited by an old family friend, my sweet mother had visited the church where Alan was pastoring. Jim, who had recently come to Christ, had begun witnessing to my dad and inviting him and my mom to visit the new church he had joined. Jim and my dad had worked together for years, and he had watched my sisters and me grow up.

As my mother's health began to deteriorate, Jim and his family began joining Alan for evening pastoral visits to our home. Alan would bring his guitar, and we would enjoy a meal together gathered around our family table. Then we would move to our large, burnt orange sectional couch. With my mom's hospice bed in the center of the room, we would sing hymns and spiritual songs. Although she was no longer able to communicate, I know these times of communion nourished her soul and encouraged her heart, especially knowing her prodigal daughter was returning to the fold.

Alan and I went on our first date the day after my mom passed on to glory. The two of us enjoyed a delightful seafood lunch at a waterfront restaurant followed by horseback riding on the beach as my heavenly Father displayed to my heart how joy and sorrow can coexist. As our friendship grew, we enjoyed soul-refreshing talks about Scripture, theology, and life, yet I was tormented as my fear of rejection grew as well. Was I safe in this relationship? Would this man I was falling in love with walk away when he discovered my rebellious past? When I decided to communicate my past failures to Alan, he responded with the same tenderness as my Savior and didn't hold my past against me. We were married eight months later.

Alan was the first man who made me feel safe and cherished. Yet throughout our thirty-plus years of marriage, I've had to learn that, though he is my greatest earthly blessing, my relationship with Christ must come first. If we put our hope in our spouse for our ultimate safety, we will become disillusioned, because they cannot be with us 24-7. There were times when Alan was out of the country on mission trips when emergencies would come up with one of our kids. I had to learn to go directly to my heavenly Father for comfort and guidance when my husband wasn't available. I am secure in Alan's love for me, but my identity is found as God's daughter, not as Alan's wife. This allows me to feel safe in my marriage, even amid occasional disagreements, because I put my hope and trust in my heavenly Father's love for me, not my amazing but fallible man. Like Abigail, I experience significance and shelter in God. You can too, dear reader, by continuing to embrace the words of Deuteronomy 33:12, which says you are beloved of the Lord and that God promises to shield you all day long.

Last, I encourage you to remember that even if you are rejected by your earthly father or husband, you are securely held by your heavenly Father!

Am I Safe in This Relationship?

My friend Michelle Ruddell learned to draw strength and courage from Christ's comforting grace after the tragic death of her five-year-old son in a car accident. In her book *Welcome to the Club—I'm Sorry You're Here: Hope for Grieving Parents*, she helps grief-stricken parents see how joy and sorrow can coexist. Below, Michelle tells the story of how Jesus delivered her from an abusive marriage after her son's devastating death—and how she found safety in her heavenly Father's embrace.

> The question in my mind was no longer *if* he would kill me, but *when*. I wasn't safe in my own home. The man who had promised to love me belittled and beat me instead.
>
> I did my best to keep the secret by covering bruises and smiling through fear. I'd married him twice. If I divorced him again, people would think I was stupid. I felt trapped.
>
> During our second marriage, our five-year-old son, Matthew, was killed in a car accident. As a new normal surfaced after that wreck, I noticed I was less afraid. *I've faced and survived the death of my son. Nothing else scares me anymore.*
>
> Slowly, I began to have a new perspective on the chaos in my life. One day my three-year-old daughter, Missy, asked me, "Is my daddy gonna kill you?" It was a pivotal moment. *I have a choice to stay in this situation or to leave. My daughters do not.*

In January 1997, my husband told me he wasn't happy in our marriage. He asked what I thought we should do. I worded my answer carefully. "I love you. I want us to raise our daughters together, but the hitting must stop." His callous response as he walked out of the room was, "I can't promise you that." The conversation was over.

I knelt in front of the couch. *God, I need Your help. I know that divorce was not Your original design for us, but neither is living like this. Please forgive me for the ways I've turned my back on You. Please show me what to do.*

From January to March, I looked for a reason to stay, anything positive, and listened for God's guidance. His answer came on March 30, 1997, Easter Sunday. After a physical altercation that morning that left me with bruises, God made it clear it was time to leave. My husband did not make any attempt to stop me. I filed charges against him that day, and he was arrested. I was free.

That escape was my Easter miracle. God spoke clearly. He provided the courage to see the charges through all the way to prosecution. Later, on a jail visit to work out divorce details, I asked my husband, "Why didn't you come after me like the other times I tried to leave?" His answer was, "I never knew you were gone."

This man who had controlled every aspect of my life never knew I had walked out that day until the police showed up to arrest him. God blinded him to the fact that I was gone.

After his arrest, I experienced unfamiliar freedom. My home wasn't scary anymore. I turned to God in gratitude and begged for his forgiveness. My daughters and I began to attend a local church. The people there loved and discipled us.

A few years later, the Easter service included a detailed description of Jesus's crucifixion. I wept as I listened. My Savior was mocked. Beaten. Spit on. He endured that willingly for me. There is nothing I have experienced that He has not suffered. I have safety in Him because He knows me and loves me. I am secure in His love and my identity as His daughter.

Finding Safe Shelter in God's Embrace

Dear reader, I pray Michelle's story encourages you. As in Abigail's story of finding safety, security, and deliverance from a toxic marriage, God supernaturally intervened in Michelle's life, helping her find identity and shelter in Him. He shielded her and her precious daughters so they could make their escape. Likewise, our heavenly Father has helped me experience safety in all my relationships, and He wants the same for you.

We all must take inventory of our associations and ask for God's wisdom in prayer. If a current relationship is unhealthy spiritually or emotionally, it's time to seek the Lord about how to confront the situation in a God-honoring way. He is steadfast in showing us when we need to break ties, and He faithfully reveals to us the path forward into healthy bonds.

Also, if you or someone you know is being physically abused, it's imperative to find secure shelter and get aid from a safe Christian community to help navigate the situation. Please see the resources provided at the end of this book.

Remember, there are no perfect friendships or marriages, and we can't expect people to meet all our needs. But our heavenly Father does want us to feel safe in our homes, churches, and friend groups. As we grow in our understanding of who God is and who we are, we can discover healthy and functional relationships.

A Prayer for His Beloved

Dear heavenly Father, I praise You for the safety and shelter You provide for Your children. I pray I would understand my identity as Your beloved. I pray You will show me any relationships I have that are unhealthy or unsafe. Please give me the discernment You gave Abigail in how to find safety for herself and her family. Please shelter me the way You helped Michelle find safety for herself and her girls, hiding them from danger. Father, show me who You are and who I am, and may I find my strength in You. I thank You for how You preserved my life, and I ask You to use my story to help others find freedom. In Jesus's name, amen.

Am I Safe in This Relationship?

Questions for Reflection

1. Describe a time you felt unsafe in a relationship. Do you see how insecurity in your identity led you to unhealthy friendships or relationships?
2. Read 1 John 3:2. What do these verses tell you about the *already* and *not yet* of your identity as God's beloved?
3. Read Psalm 118:8. Where are you to put your trust, and where should you find refuge?
4. Using Ephesians 5: 6–10 as a guide, ask God to give you the wisdom and discernment He gave Abigail to navigate any abusive or unhealthy relationships.
5. How have unhealthy relationships held you back in ministry? What is a practical step you can take today to establish God-honoring boundaries?

Chapter Three

Will I Ever Find Acceptance?

To the praise of the glory of His grace, by which
He made us accepted in the Beloved.

EPHESIANS 1:6 NKJV

"I believe Mark is missing out on God's best for him."

It was soul-crushing hearing those words had been spoken about me. I wasn't God's best for Mark? I was nineteen years old and dating a navy pilot. He was obviously brilliant, as he was number one in his class. Yet feelings of inferiority and fear of not being accepted by his tribe exacerbated my shyness and social anxiety. Mark and I had been together for about a year when I was introduced to a large group of his family members at his winging ceremony, where student naval aviators receive their wings of gold after completing military flight training. It was a fun evening filled with celebration and dancing, and the cocktails flowed freely.

Yet my fears of not being accepted were realized the next day when I found out Mark's aunt had said those words about our

47

relationship. Her comment was meant to attack my "worldliness"—I wasn't godly enough for her dear nephew. I was indeed backslidden at the time and not living according to the faith I had professed in middle school, but Mark was not living out his Christian profession at the time either. Yet I took the brunt of the judgment.

My insecurity was compounded by comments made by his younger sister, with whom he was very close. She had not been able to attend the winging ceremony, but in a congratulatory phone call to her brother, she pointed out our families' different socioeconomic and educational backgrounds. As a sociology major, she referred to these as factors leading to unsuccessful marriages. I interpreted her viewpoint to mean I was not cultured enough for her brother.

Not all of his family responded in negative ways. Mark's mother was kind and accepting of me. Even after Mark and I broke up, she wrote me a lovely note when I lost my mother to cancer.

It's easy to say his aunt and sister should have reached out to me with grace and shared truth in love instead of casting a condemning attitude. Yet I know I have done the same thing to others in the past. We all need God's grace and truth. I love Rosaria Butterfield's thoughts on responding to other people's sins. Rosaria, who lived as a practicing lesbian before her conversion, said, "Some say you should love the sinner and hate the sin. I think we should love the sinner and hate our own sin. If we spent more time hating our own sin, we would be more responsible in our dealings with others."[5]

Yes, I agree with Rosaria. When I take time to contemplate the depths of my own sin and the incredible grace and forgiveness Christ has shown me, it gives me compassion in my responses to others.

I write more about my return to the faith and then marrying my husband, a pastor, in another chapter. Yet that joyful transformation in my life did not end my incessant striving for approval and validation. I just transitioned my efforts to church life, where I often felt unworthy as a pastor's wife. It may appear more noble when we try and prove ourselves through Christian service, but the discouragement and disillusionment it leads to are the same.

Have you ever felt like you don't measure up or fit in? Or that you must change who you are to gain the acceptance of a group? I spent much of my life striving to find my identity through the acceptance of others. The problem—people are fickle. What gains their acceptance one day earns their disapproval the next. Friend, if you endeavor to find approval and security through other people's opinions of you, whether in the church or in the world, it is a vicious cycle that only leads to greater insecurity. As Christ-followers, we are accepted in the Beloved—His Son, Jesus. Ultimately, His is the only approval we need.

The Sinful Woman

> And behold, a woman of the city, who was a sinner, when she learned that he was reclining at table in the Pharisee's house, brought an alabaster flask of ointment, and standing behind him at his feet, weeping, she began to wet his feet with her tears and wiped them with the hair of her head and kissed his feet and anointed them with the ointment. **(Luke 7:37–38)**

The sinful woman in Luke 7 found acceptance in the Beloved. Some commentators believe this woman to be Mary Magdalene. However, I agree with theologian Charles Spurgeon who said, "This is the woman who has been confounded with Mary Magdalene. How the error originated, would not be easy to imagine, but an error it certainly is. There is not the slightest shadow of evidence that this woman, who was a sinner, had even the remotest connection with her out of whom Jesus cast seven devils."[6]

Spurgeon did not believe there was adequate proof from the account in Luke 7 to show this to be Mary Magdalene. Nor was this Mary of Bethany. Mary, the sister of Martha and Lazarus, did anoint her Savior in a separate account six days before the Passover and just before Jesus's triumphal entry. However, this woman in Luke 7 interrupted a dinner party at Simon the Pharisee's house and began anointing and kissing Jesus's feet, wetting them with her tears, and drying them with her hair. Named only as a sinner, some commentators believe she was a prostitute. If this were true, she would have been considered untouchable by the religious rulers. Simon the Pharisee, who was the dinner host, revealed his feelings about this anointing occurring in his home. "If this man were a prophet, he would have known who and what sort of woman this is who is touching him, for she is a sinner" (Luke 7:39). Through his contempt, we see her unacceptance in civilized society. This Pharisee calls into question Jesus's authority when he says that if Jesus were a true prophet, he would know the identity of this woman as a sinner.

In Luke 7:41–50, we learn that the Savior responded to the host's disdain with a parable. Jesus tells the story of a moneylender and two people who owed him money. One of the debtors owed five hundred denarii, and the other owed fifty. When neither of them could pay the moneylender what they owed, he forgave the debt for both. After telling this story, Jesus asked the self-righteous Simon which one of the debtors would love the moneylender more. Simon answered that he supposed it would be the one for whom he canceled the larger debt. Jesus told Simon he had answered correctly and then turned to the woman and praised her sacrificial show of love and worship. Jesus described in detail how the woman had washed His feet with her tears, dried them with her hair, and anointed His feet with ointment. Jesus then says, "'Therefore I tell you, her sins, which are many, are forgiven—for she loved much. But he who is forgiven little, loves little.' And he said to her, 'Your sins are forgiven'" (Luke 7:47–48). The one who was forgiven the greater debt is the one who loved most.

So does this mean my husband, who did not fall into the same sins and snares I did growing up, does not love Jesus as much as I do because I had more that needed to be forgiven? If we look at it that way, we are missing the point. Let's look at Luke 5:31–32 for further insight. "And Jesus answered them, 'Those who are well have no need of a physician, but those who are sick. I have not come to call the righteous but sinners to repentance.'" I believe this passage is saying that those who don't recognize their sin-sickness and their need for a physician, like the pharisaical Simon, are self-righteous, seeing no need for the sacrificial death of Christ. We see a clear difference in the sinful woman who, in humility and sorrow, recognized her need for Christ's forgiveness. Jesus finishes this lesson to the dinner crowd by telling Simon the Pharisee that the woman's many sins are forgiven because of her profound display of love.

This dear woman could have permitted the looks of disdain from the others to cause her to retreat before she finished her act of love to the Savior. Or she could have made the excuse that she wanted to wait to come to Jesus after she found acceptance among the religious leaders. But, instead, she humbly worshipped and served the Savior for all to see. And then something beautiful happened—

Jesus spoke directly to her and forgave her sins. She found acceptance in the Beloved! Her identity was not the sinful woman—she was the daughter of the King. Likewise, we must remember that when we find our acceptance in Christ, we worship and serve an audience of one and can release the need for approval from other people.

Grace Draws Us in, Truth Sets Us Free

I have heard people say, "Jesus accepts everyone just as they are." While it's true that Jesus does not expect us to clean ourselves up before we come to Him, that does not mean He *accepts* our sin. He *receives* our sin upon Himself when we ask for forgiveness and put our faith in His work on the cross. I once heard a speaker say the following regarding our outreach to those caught in a lifestyle contrary to God's Word: "Grace draws them in, but truth sets them free." There is no true freedom and change without confronting ourselves and others with the truth. Grace without truth is ineffective, and truth without grace is ugly! We must share the gospel with truth and grace, reaching out to the outcasts in our society and showing them how to receive lasting acceptance in Christ.

Some have experienced rejection by the world yet have not lived a lifestyle like the sinful woman in Luke 7. My friend Christina England tells the story of striving for acceptance as a professional singer, only to be judged on appearance instead of her incredible talent. But she finally found acceptance in her heavenly Father, who revealed His plan for her to use her voice for Him.

> My whole life, I have sought an extra portion of acceptance and attention by using my voice. At a

very young age, I put a milk crate in the middle of our street, stood on it, and sang to oncoming traffic. Because of the deep ditches on each side of the road, cars could not go around me. I guess you could say it was a guaranteed captivated audience! Working on a vehicle in the garage, my dad noticed what was happening and swooped me and my stage off the street. That was not where I belonged. Although my parents loved me fully, I had this insatiable desire for more. Choose me, pick me, notice me, pay attention to me. In elementary school, I was the chubby, awkward weirdo affectionately called by my last name. I never fit in and was frequently left out.

Growing up, our enormous family had a cabin on a lake. Cousins would pile in the back of a van while other vehicles hauled suitcases to the best memory-making destination ever. One trip etched in my memory was when I sang "Delta Dawn," by Tanya Tucker, over and over and over and over. My cousins were yelling at me to shut up, eventually smothering me with pillows to make me stop. That was not the encore response I was looking for!

In my freshman year of high school, we moved from Texas to Michigan, and the transition was hard. Finding my people seemed impossible, and I didn't feel very welcome at my new school. I was first chair alto saxophone in Austin, but the band director in Michigan wouldn't let me try out for marching band.

Instead, he pushed me aside and into concert band. But sometime after that, a new opportunity opened.

Although I had never done anything like it, I decided to try out for the school musical. After my audition, Mr. DeMaria, the choir director, pulled me aside and invited me to join the choir. He encouraged me to transfer from band to choir the following semester. Finally, I was excited to be welcomed somewhere with open arms and truly enjoyed Acapella Choir and Madrigals! Throughout high school, I tried out for every solo offered and received more than my fair share. I clearly remember another choir teacher reminding me that it was time to give someone else a chance. But I was just thrilled that I had finally found acceptance. My excitement grew even more when the opportunity to audition for show choir arose, and I thought, *Yes, yes, yes! This is where I'm meant to be.* However, I was shocked, and my soul was crushed when I was told no. The only explanation was that I "wasn't a good fit." In my heart, I believed it was because I was the weird, chubby girl and wondered why I had ever let myself believe I would fit in.

In college, I allowed myself to hope again. Believing I could find acceptance as a vocal music performance major, I immediately dove into the entry-level show choir. This was the most fun I'd ever had. Every semester there were open auditions for the premier show choir. These shows were top-notch and spectacular in every way, and I desperately wanted to be a part of them. So I poured my heart and soul into preparing for the audition. My confidence was crushed when I didn't make the cut. My show choir teacher read me the feedback from the panel of vocal music department professors. I don't remember the exact words, but essentially, they said, "Singing voice 10, looks 3." My teacher gently encouraged me to try losing some weight. I didn't dare tell her I was the thinnest I'd ever been since I hit my teens. Instead, feeling rejected again, I turned away and soon dropped out of college.

The passion for the stage still burned within my heart, so I worked up the courage and competed in local contests. I even became well-known in our region. In 1996, I earned a spot to perform in a showcase competition at the Grand Ole Opry! It was an invigorating time. One after another, for two straight days, vocalists performed their songs in the circle where countless music legends had before. Next, we were ranked and given written feedback from the panel of judges. My rank? Thirteenth place out of hundreds! However, my hopes were once again dashed when I read the only negative comments. The negative feedback was not constructive and basically told me I was too fat to make it in their world. I wasn't their kind. I once again felt unaccepted.

Two months after that painful rejection, a major radio station announced a singing competition. The winner would sing a solo at the Jimmy Buffet concert. I sent my demo to the radio station, thinking *this* could be the big break I was looking for. I was thrilled when my name was one of ten that they announced to go backstage for an audition before Jimmy Buffet's band. Once at the venue, we learned the song we had to sing to a crowd of over 10,000 people. I stepped onto that stage like a boss and began singing the song they chose for me, and soon the crowd was cheering and singing with me. They loved me, and I won the contest! Yet, strangely, the thrill didn't last, as I soon realized it didn't bring me the security and significance I thought it would. Deep down, I knew this wasn't my place.

Shortly after that experience, life took an unexpected turn, and God intervened. My heavenly Father now had my full attention, and I chose to stop pursuing a music career in the secular world. He showed me I would never find my identity and significance on the stage I had fought so hard to stand on. All the years of striving for acceptance had only been a distraction that lured me away from what God had in store.

I am reminded of the sinful woman in the Bible who found acceptance in the Beloved through a humble act of faith and worship. Her identity changed from *sinful woman* to *servant of Christ*. She was rejected by the religious community because of her sin. I was rejected by the musical performance community because I didn't have the look they wanted. Whatever the reason for the rejection we experience, the pain is the same, and so is the answer. We each must find acceptance and validation from God and understand our identity as His daughter.

The sinful woman found acceptance by God by worshipping and serving King Jesus before a dinner party. I found acceptance by serving Him as a worship leader, and my identity changed from *weirdo fat girl* to *daughter of King Jesus*. You see, eight years later, my feet were placed on a sanctuary platform for the first time, and I knew I was where I was meant to be. What a privilege it is to use my voice to lead others in the worship of our King. I now stand on God's stage, which is secure and significant!

You Are God's Masterpiece

What about you, dear reader? If you are tired of striving yet never receiving the prize, I hope Christina's story encourages you. I invite you to step off the performance treadmill and break the power of other people's opinions. Jesus accomplished what you can never accomplish for yourself so that you could rest in His finished work. Let's think about Ephesians 2:10 again. "For we are his workmanship, created in Christ Jesus for good works, which God prepared beforehand, that we should walk in them." We don't have to work to discover our identity. This verse tells us who we are—God's workmanship and masterpiece. Likewise, we don't have to find our purpose—we were created in Christ Jesus for good works. If you're wondering what those good works look like for you, ask your heavenly Father because He is the one who prepared them for you! Like my friend Christina, who found her place on God's stage and the sinful woman who found her seat at Jesus's feet, let's joyfully serve our Father in the space He has created for us. As Christ-followers, we are accepted in the Beloved, His Son, Jesus. Ultimately, His is the only approval we need.

I encourage you to write the following on a notecard and place it where you can see it: My name is _____. My identity is Daughter of the King, Child of God, and Servant of Christ. I no longer need to strive for approval because I am accepted in the Beloved!

A Prayer for His Beloved

Dear heavenly Father, I praise You for Your glorious grace, which makes us accepted in the Beloved. I pray I will understand that You did not come to call the righteous, but You came to call sinners to repentance. May I experience the power of Your grace in new and fresh ways, just as the sinful woman did. May I love You and others much because I have been forgiven much. Father, please reveal to me if I am striving for acceptance from people, either in the world or in the church, instead of resting in the acceptance I have in You. Father, in humility and love, may I worship You with abandonment, as the sinful woman did. May I stay in the lane that You have paved for me, releasing my need for approval from others. Father, may I know I serve an audience of one! In Jesus's name, amen.

Questions for Reflection

1. Describe a time you did not feel accepted.
2. Describe a time someone showed you truth without grace or grace without truth.
3. Read John 19:11. What do you think this verse teaches about sin?
4. Read John 6:37. What comfort does this verse give Christ-followers regarding our acceptance by God the Father, through Christ Jesus, despite what we've done or will do?
5. Read Romans 14:1–2. What do these verses tell us about accepting those who are weaker in their faith or have different convictions on nonessentials than we do?
6. Read Ephesians 2:10. What does this verse show you about your calling?
7. How are you allowing fear of not being accepted hold you back in ministry? What practical step can you take today to move forward and serve an audience of one?

Chapter Four

Where Do I Find Deliverance?

There are two equal and opposite errors into which our race can fall about the devils. One is to disbelieve in their existence. The other is to believe and to feel an excessive and unhealthy interest in them. They themselves are equally pleased by both errors and hail a materialist or a magician with the same delight.

—C. S. LEWIS[7]

Sitting in the worship gathering at the church my husband was pastoring, I earnestly interceded and claimed the shed blood of Jesus over my mind and body. I silently but boldly declared, *I am a child of God; you have no power over me!* Then my body began to tremble as I called upon God the Father to glorify His name in my affliction. On the heels of that silent prayer, my dear pastor and husband read: "'Father, glorify your name!' Then a voice came from heaven, 'I have glorified it, and will glorify it again'" (John 12:28 NIV). Contemplating that moment still gives me chills. After he read John 12:28, the oppression intensified, and I could feel my body begin to crumble. I stumbled to the sanctuary door to make my escape. I fell in the hallway, and my water bottle bounced onto the tile floor, causing a cacophony of sound.

Faithful friends leaped from their seats to help me into the church library. I was told my eyes rolled back in my head and that deep guttural sounds escaped from my throat as my limbs jerked uncontrollably. It appeared to my helpers that I experienced a grand mal seizure. Some years earlier, when my bizarre symptoms began, the neurologists referred to them as pseudoseizures when my tests came back within the normal range. However, that term is no longer medically correct. *Nonepileptic seizure* or a *nonepileptic event* is currently considered the correct term. Some doctors believe the symptoms manifest from not recognizing or responding to an emotional conflict, so I began to ponder where my mental health struggles, physical symptoms, and spiritual oppression intersected. I discovered there was no simple answer.

The first several years of my affliction were spent obsessing over the physical. I desperately sought an organic diagnosis, feeling driven to prove to the medical community that I wasn't crazy. I was a Christian, a pastor's wife, and a Bible study teacher. How could I possibly have mental health issues that would manifest in such an extreme way? Also, I couldn't comprehend how spiritual oppression could affect a born-again believer in such a fashion. However, through prayer and the study of Scripture, I began to accept that people in ministry are not exempt from mental health struggles. The Enemy indeed attacks those in kingdom-work with a vengeance. The road to healing began when I acknowledged that my past was affecting my present.

What about you? Have you ever felt like there is a battlefield of negative thoughts and accusations waging war in your mind? Perhaps you or someone you know wrestles with unexplained and perplexing physical health issues. I've seen the Enemy use unprocessed trauma to wreak havoc in my life and the lives of my loved ones. God's Word tells us, however, that He sent His Son to set the captives free! The good news is that our heavenly Father wants to restore our peace and joy as we process and release the pain of our past.

Because unprocessed trauma or grief can lead to unforgiveness— which can give the Enemy an area of entry to cause spiritual oppression—this is a confusing and complex topic. (Note that Scripture calls Satan "the author of confusion.") We know our fierce yet tender heavenly Father does not want us confused or fearful of the devil or his hosts. I encourage you to go back and read the C. S. Lewis quote at the beginning of this chapter. Lewis warns us against being ignorant of the devil's schemes and ignoring his existence, while also not obsessing over the demonic and seeing a demon behind every problem. If we are ignorant of the Enemy's tactics, we will not develop an effective battle plan for living in victory. And if we blame everything wrong in our lives on the Enemy, we minimize God's sovereignty and live as a victim instead of a victor. An obsessive interest in the demonic draws our eyes away from Christ Jesus and leads to fear and anxiety.

Addressing Unhealed Wounds

In her book *Forgiving My Father, Forgiving Myself*, Billy Graham's daughter Ruth Graham talks about wrestling through trauma and forgiveness after her husband's affair. She explains that, until that point, she had a superficial view of forgiveness and had treated unforgiveness as an emotion to bury. She says,

> And since I was a master at masking my negative feelings, even from myself, whenever I encountered a need to give forgiveness, I'd been satisfied to pray, meditate on some forgiveness verses, and then do my best to forget my pain. I believed the old saying that "time heals all wounds." Little did I know that, in truth, time buries all wounds that are not dealt with, and such wounds are buried alive. So, buried they remained, securely tucked away beneath my layers of denial and repression until I experienced a life-altering trauma.[8]

If we deny or repress our pain by merely slapping a Bible verse on the situation and moving on, we aren't truly experiencing the miracle of forgiveness. Burying the trauma while it is still throbbing will only cause it to erupt from beneath the surface when we encounter another wounding. Unprocessed trauma leads to unforgiveness, which can enable a root of bitterness to grow in the darkness under the veneer of our carefully planned lives, making us susceptible to demonic oppression. Ephesians 4:26–27 says, "Be angry and do not sin; do not let the sun go down on your anger, and give no opportunity to the devil." This verse tells us it's normal to experience anger when we are sinned against. But anger is an emotion that needs to be addressed and processed according to the instructions given in Scripture. Because if we plant and fertilize anger, we unknowingly give the devil a point of entry.

Digging deeper into my past, I thought about being raised in a dysfunctional home by two parents who loved me but were products of their own dysfunctional upbringing. I grew up with incredible insecurity, crippling anxiety, and overwhelming shyness that followed me into my early adulthood. The loneliness, fear, and isolation I experienced as a child left me vulnerable to the lies of the Enemy of my soul. I believed in his slanderous words that I was unworthy and stupid and would never receive unconditional love. These deep-seated lies led to my experimenting with drugs and abusing alcohol in my teen years to mask the pain and anxiety. And before that, I was so consumed with people-pleasing and fear of rejection that I participated in a séance at party in middle school. My reckless decisions did not give the Evil One possession of my soul, but my sin, unbelief, and the opening of demonic portals did lead to extreme oppression. As I unknowingly took the Enemy's lies to heart, the truths of what Christ said about me in His Word were more head knowledge than heart knowledge. Because when we don't know who we are, we are susceptible to the Enemy's lies.

What about you? Do you truly grasp the tender love and care of your heavenly Father and your identity as His child? If we do not fully get the Father's love and care, we will not live confidently in our identity but will continually strive to prove ourselves worthy. We will likewise unknowingly bury our wounds, failing to live as forgiven children and not extending forgiveness to others, which makes us vulnerable to Satan's deception. Remember, we are not responsible for the lies he tells us, but we are responsible for believing them.

As explained in her book, Ruth Graham says, "Bitterness always bears fruit. It may take years to reveal itself. But it will. As Hebrews 12:15 warns, bitterness can grow a root that, when it springs up, will cause trouble, and many will be defiled by it."[9]

I realized I was still holding onto bitterness toward my dad for childhood wounds. This affected my marriage and ministry and caused trouble and damage to my four children. Yet through recognition, confession, and prayer, our heavenly Father is "restoring the years the locusts have eaten" (Joel 2:25). Through the power of Jesus, our family is breaking generational patterns and tearing down strongholds.

Oppressed by the Enemy

> *Soon afterward he went on through cities and villages, proclaiming and bringing the good news of the kingdom of God. And the twelve were with him, and also some women who had been healed of evil spirits and infirmities: Mary, called Magdalene, from whom seven demons had gone out, and Joanna, the wife of Chuza, Herod's household manager, and Susanna, and many others, who provided for them out of their means.* **Luke 8:1–3**

Mary Magdalene is a biblical example of oppression by the Evil One. We do not know a whole lot about her. Mary Magdalene is mentioned in all four Gospels as a witness to the crucifixion and empty tomb. In Matthew and John, she also encounters the resurrected Jesus. Only in Luke is Mary mentioned before the crucifixion. Luke 8 lists Mary Magdalene as one of several women who traveled with

Jesus and the disciples in Galilee. And we read she was healed of evil spirits and had seven demons cast out of her.

What events led to Mary's demonic oppression? We do not know, as Scripture does not tell us. As mentioned in chapter 2, some believe Mary Magdalene is the "sinful woman" who washed and anointed Jesus's feet in Luke 7. But there is no proof that this is the same woman. And there is strong reason to believe the sinful woman spoken of in Luke is a prostitute, yet there is no proof that Mary Magdalene was a prostitute.

Spurgeon said the following about her:

> We are never told of her that she was a great sinner; in fact, not a word is said against her personal character; we are simply informed that she was possessed with seven devils, which is an affliction rather than a crime. I do not deny that sin may have prepared her for the satanic possession and was no doubt also occasioned by it, but she is not brought before us in Scripture as a transgressor, nor is she the representative of great offenders, but rather the type of a class of persons who for years are sore vexed in heart, greatly depressed in spirit, heavily burdened with despondency."[10]

Spurgeon says we have no scriptural proof that Satan possessed Mary Magdalene due to her having an evil character. However, her personal sin could have magnified her affliction. I believe she was held captive by the Enemy's lies until Jesus cast out the seven demons vexing her, which enabled her to realize her identity in her deliverer. Colossians 1:13 says, "He has delivered us from the domain of darkness and transferred us to the kingdom of his beloved Son." Jesus brings the same deliverance from oppression to us as we release the darkness of unprocessed wounds and unforgiveness and realize our position in His kingdom.

We know Mary Magdalene discovered her identity and purpose because Luke 8:1–2 says she traveled with Jesus and the disciples as they shared the good news of the gospel, going through cities and villages together. Mary, the social outcast held captive by seven demons, now accompanied the Savior in ministry and helped provide for His needs out of her means. Friend, your past, no matter how ugly or painful, does not disqualify you from ministry. I, the party girl turned pastor's wife, am a trophy of God's grace!

We Have a Good, Good Father

Like with Mary Magdalene, the Enemy may have a plan against you and me, and he is mighty. But God is almighty! That morning I experienced a seizure in church, I began a series of several prayer meetings interceding for my deliverance from the lies I believed, due to buried wounds and unforgiveness. The final session was with a therapist and a dear friend. They both battled with me in prayer, rebuking the lies the Enemy spewed forth through my mouth and replacing them with the truth of what the Father said about me, His blood-bought daughter.

A dear pastor and friend of ours, Charley Chase, has written a book about the love and goodness our heavenly Father extends to us as His children. In his book *Good, Good Father: Knowing God as He Wants to Be Known*, Chase writes, "His predestining you before creation came from his pre-creation love for you. The Father has always loved you individually, you in the deep DNA sense that makes you—you. Your heavenly Father loves you eternally."[11]

Our heavenly Father had a pre-creation love for us as Christ-followers. Before we were formed in our mother's womb, His eternal love drove Him to bridge the sin gap between us. Ephesians 1:5–6 says, "In love, he predestined us for adoption to Himself as sons through Jesus Christ, according to the purpose of his will, to the praise of his glorious grace, with which he has blessed us in the Beloved." Friend, I encourage you to spend some time resting in your heavenly Father's pre-creation, predestinating love that provided a way for your adoption and deliverance through His glorious grace. Together, let us give praise for our blessings in the Beloved, who is our Savior, Christ Jesus. This eternal love provided a way to restore the intimate relationship and fellowship our Father longs for us to enjoy with Him.

Ruth Graham wrote of how she realized her core issue was feelings of abandonment, which led to unforgiveness and poor relationship choices. While talking to a good friend about all the relationship mistakes she had made, Ruth's friend provided deep insight:

> He looked into my eyes and said, 'You felt abandoned as a child.' My eyes suddenly filled with tears, and I instantly knew he had hit a nerve. He had spoken truth. I did not want to admit it and tried to hide it, but he was right. I recognized the truth deep down in the dark recesses of my heart. Yes, my core issue is abandonment."[12]

Once Ruth could see the root of her unprocessed wound and the unforgiveness she was carrying, true healing began to take place in her life. She was able to put a stop to the Enemy's lies she had unknowingly believed. The same was true for me and can be true for you too.

As a pastor's wife and Bible teacher, I understood Jesus loved me and died for my sins, and I had the intellectual asset of my acceptance by God the Father through Christ's blood. But I had a disconnect in my understanding of God's eternal, unconditional, and tender love for me as His daughter. My core issue stemmed from my complex relationship with my flawed earthly father. I was transferring a performance-based love and acceptance into my relationship with my heavenly Father. I likewise realized I had a root of bitterness toward my earthly father that needed to be uprooted and destroyed to fully experience the miracle of forgiveness—to be delivered.

There is still mystery regarding where the physical, mental-emotional, and spiritual aspects of my story collide or divide. We are created with a body, mind, and spirit. A beautiful Creator is so intertwined in all three areas that it is hard to know where one ends and another begins. After years of suffering, I realized my issues were threefold: physical, emotional, and spiritual. I have had to address each facet.

Physically, I have an autoimmune disease with measurable symptoms, for which I undergo monthly treatments. Separately, my current neurologist believes I have epileptic and nonepileptic seizures and has me on an anticonvulsant.

Emotionally and mentally, I wrestle with anxiety, which is now controlled through psychotherapy and medication. I've also done eye movement desensitization and reprocessing (EMDR) therapy. I have painstakingly cleaned out old wounds and reprocessed traumatic memories.

Spiritually, I've discovered the Enemy's lies are at the root of all my unresolved wounds and traumatic memories. The same is valid for sins that I've struggled to break free from. Returning and addressing the lies and replacing them with the truths of Scripture closes the door to any access the Enemy has gained in my life. The freedom, peace, victory, and soul restoration this painful process brings is glorious.

The same can be true of you, dear reader. Help, hope, and healing are your portion as well. In Deuteronomy 33:12 (NIV), Moses addressed the twelve tribes of Israel. About Benjamin, he said, "Let the beloved of the Lord rest secure in him, for he shields him all day long, and the one the Lord loves, rests between his shoulders." I pray that as a Christ-follower, you begin to grasp what it means to be beloved of the Lord. I pray you realize your past sin and failure do not prevent you from walking with Jesus or disqualify you from service—quite the opposite!

Your identity is secure. God is your shield and the lifter of your head despite any physical ailments or daily battles you face. In Him you are safe and protected from the Enemy's attacks on your soul. You can climb up on your heavenly Daddy's back and find physical, emotional, and spiritual rest between His shoulders and claim the promise found in 1 Peter 5:10: "And after you have suffered a little while, the God of all grace, who has called you to his eternal glory in Christ, will himself restore, confirm, strengthen, and establish you."

A Prayer for His Beloved

Dear heavenly Father, I praise You for Your pre-creation, predestinating love. I pray I will understand the vastness of Your eternal affections for me. I pray You will show me where to turn for help and healing for unprocessed wounds or areas of unforgiveness. I praise You for the deliverance the cross has already provided for me. May I remember that we don't fight for victory but from victory.

Father, help me take up the shield of faith and extinguish the lies the Enemy shoots at me. May I take up the sword of the Spirit, the Word of God, and replace the lies with the truths in the Scriptures. Like Mary Magdalene, may I minister alongside Your Son, walking out my calling through my blood-bought freedom.

Finally, I claim the promise found in Romans 16:20: "The God of peace will soon crush Satan under your feet. The grace of our Lord Jesus Christ be with you." Amen.

Questions for Reflection

1. Describe a time you felt tortured by your thoughts. Have you considered that you may have unprocessed wounds?
2. Read Hebrews 12:15. What does it tell us about the root of bitterness?
3. Read Joel 2:25. God wants you to live healed and be a change agent for the next generation. What does He promise in Joel?
4. Read Ephesians 1:4–5. When did God's love for you begin? How did He express the depths of His love to you individually?
5. Read Luke 8:1–3. After gaining freedom from oppression, what did Mary Magdalene do?
6. How are you allowing your past to hold you back in ministry? What is a practical step you can take today to move forward?

Finding our Significance in God's Embrace

Chapter Five

Why Do I Still Feel Shame?

My memory is nearly gone, but I remember two things: that I am a great sinner, and that Christ is a great Savior.

—JOHN NEWTON

"She's pottying; she's pottying!" James, a boy with special needs in my first-grade class, was pointing at me and excitingly flapping his arms and crying out those words. Simultaneously the warm liquid soaked my bottom and ran off my chair, forming a puddle of shame beneath me. James and I were the only two students from our class sitting in the speech lab while our peers were at recess. We were with a group of primary students with speech impediments, each with inflexible black earphones curved over our heads and connected by a thin wire to an audio source. We were listening to the proper way to pronounce digraphs while the laughter of our classmates echoed outside on the playground.

Our peers enjoyed pumping their legs with gusto on the belt swings in hopes of their feet reaching the sky and spinning on the merry-go-round until their tummies were woozy in the hot Texas sun. Of course, they all survived the merry-go-round madness, an experience our grandkids will never have as the safety police have ripped out most of them from modern playgrounds!

Back in the speech room, I felt lightheaded, but not from the merry-go-round. Startled by James's shouts, the teacher's aide, eyes wide with surprise, came running over to my chair. With quivering lips and head bowed in humiliation and fear, I nervously repeated, "I'm so sorry, I'm so sorry!" Miss Carter hurriedly began grabbing some towels out of a cupboard and assured me I wasn't in trouble. But then she told me I would need to go and find my teacher on the playground and tell her what happened.

When I finally stood up from my sticky, soppy mess, my thin, long legs trembled as I began my trail of shame to the playground. Thankfully, when I found my teacher, the moment was handled discreetly, and someone accompanied me to the classroom to find a clean pair of paisley-print pink shorts from the extra clothes bag for emergencies. (Rose-colored Barbie shorts take the edge off a traumatic experience!)

I didn't wet my pants in the first grade because I had bladder control issues but rather because I was too shy to tell my teacher I needed to use the restroom before class. Also, the fear of getting chastised always loomed large for me, and I was afraid I would get in trouble if I removed my headphones in the middle of the lesson. Likewise, I dreaded making my way to the front of the speech lab by myself. From an early age, I was not too fond of the spotlight, yet I longed to be received in a group. I wanted to always stay under the radar, yet I simultaneously longed to be seen.

As a small child, I remember yearning to be embraced like my younger sister Lori. She was an adorable blond with light green eyes, full of spunk and personality. All our adult cousins on my dad's side adored her affectionate nature. Conversely, I felt like I was invisible while Lori relished in the attention of strangers. I interpreted the lack of awareness as a sign that I was unacceptable and unlovable, not understanding that it's common for people to be drawn to a baby or toddler. I also didn't recognize how my shyness made me seem unapproachable. In shame, I thought there was something wrong with me.

Then in primary school, I was ashamed when I was the only girl in my first-grade class who had to go to the speech lab during recess. What I didn't understand at the time is that we all have some form of special needs. I know James's autism was much more life-altering than my lisp or extreme shyness, but we must realize that *invisible* special needs are no less real. Yet I decided at a young age that I would never measure up to or be accepted among the smart and popular kids—never dreaming that they had issues they wrestled with as well.

What about you? Have you ever felt shame and intense embarrassment, even if whatever you did was an accident? Or has an unwanted divorce or a painful and abrupt ending to a friendship made you feel like something is wrong with you? According to Google Dictionary, the definition of shame is, "A painful feeling of humiliation or distress caused by the consciousness of wrong or foolish behavior."[13]

What if we're feeling shame over something that was neither foolish nor wrong but was just an unfortunate accident? Or maybe we're ashamed of something that happened to us because of someone else's choice and not our own. Or maybe we're feeling shame over something that wasn't our fault, but the perpetrator conditioned us to believe it was. Friend, sometimes we feel guilt or shame over something we are guilty of, but sometimes we feel false guilt and shame over something that was not in any way our fault.

Perhaps, like me, you must do soul work to understand why the lines are blurred. I'm not throwing my parents under the bus here—they were products of their own dysfunctional upbringing—but as a child, I would sometimes get punished for things that I did by accident. It seemed that anything I did that upset my dad was never understood or accepted as an honest mistake. He usually assigned a dishonest or impure motive to the behavior or situation. Seeds of confusion over what I was responsible for and what I wasn't were sown into my life from a young age. Again, my dad reacted and responded the way he did because he experienced trauma in his own childhood and young adult years and never received counseling.

When Daddy was a child (he was much younger than his three older siblings), his older brother Homer was killed during World War II while at sea. It is believed that Homer's ship was tragically struck by friendly fire. His body was not recovered. My dad's parents didn't know how to process the trauma with their remaining children, which included Daddy and his two older sisters. I believe they each must have felt isolated in their loss and grief as they tried to cope individually instead of as a family unit. Then years later, when my dad was a teenager—and the only child still living at home—his dog was fighting with another dog, causing his dad to yell for him to get the dogs away from each other. His father was sick in bed at the time, and the agitation caused him to go into cardiac arrest. My grandmother yelled for my dad to run and get the doctor, but by the time he returned with help, it was too late, and his father was dead. My dad carried a lot of false shame and guilt, believing his father's fatal heart attack was his fault because of his dog. The stress and trauma were compounded by a neighbor who immediately told my dad he was then the man of the house—a lot of pressure and false responsibility for a thirteen-year-old boy. As a result, my father struggled with shame and, in his adulthood, suffered mood swings and an explosive temper. He self-medicated with alcohol for many years.

Growing up, I could never seem to keep my dad's approval. After gaining it, I had to work hard to keep it. So as a teenager, I finally quit trying. Despite being known as the goody-two-shoes since childhood, in high school, I started living a double life on the weekends and engaging in the party scene.

Even after returning to the arms of my Savior as an adult, and despite being a faithful Christian, pastor's wife, and Bible teacher, I lived with shame for years. Sometimes it was over memories of my actions and choices during that season of rebellion from my high school and early college days—sins I had confessed and been forgiven of—yet I still held onto the guilt. I also struggled with shame over things I wasn't responsible for. In my mind, the lines were blurred regarding things that were my fault and things that weren't. It didn't matter if I made an honest mistake or committed sins of omission or commission, shame would plague me for days and keep me up at night. It wasn't uncommon for me to take the blame for things I shouldn't have, then allow humiliating and deeply distressing thoughts to consume me.

I viewed this as a normal conviction of sin and would either call on the phone or write letters of apology to everyone who either saw me sin or make a mistake, hoping this would help ease my conscience and distress. Conviction of sin is a gift from the Holy Spirit and is a mercy from God to keep us from continuing down a path that will lead to destruction. Shame, on the other hand, can be a tool from the Enemy to keep us distressed and stuck in despair. For example, early in our ministry, a woman once called me because I had repeated something regarding her husband's health. She informed me it was told to my husband in confidence and asked me not to repeat it again. I apologized and asked for her forgiveness, and she extended it. Even though my husband hadn't told me it was confidential, I felt I should have known better than to repeat the news. And though she told me I was forgiven, I couldn't let it go, so I wrote her husband a letter asking for his forgiveness. Still feeling guilty, I called the one person I had told and began crying on the phone, asking her forgiveness for telling her something I shouldn't have. Because I had not learned to take my thoughts captive, the Enemy kept me stuck in shame and despair for weeks.

God's Amazing Grace

John Newton (1725–1807) is the author of one of the most famous hymns of all time, "Amazing Grace." The first stanza says, "Amazing grace! How sweet the sound That saved a wretch like me! I once was lost, but now am found; Was blind, but now I see."[14]

I'm sure Newton had his past life involvement in the evil and immoral African slave trade in mind when he referred to himself as a wretch. According to Google Dictionary, a *wretch* is "a despicable or contemptible person,"[15] which Newton indeed was before he was convicted of his sin. However, when awakened to the amazing grace of God, which he later sang about, his identity changed. He could release the shame over his great sins and who he was apart from Christ and find his hope and joy in his great Savior.

The *Holman Bible Dictionary* says the following about the conviction of sin: "The conviction results in hope, not despair. Once individuals are made aware of their estranged relationship with God, they are challenged and encouraged to mend that relationship. The conviction not only implies the exposure of sin (despair) but also a call to repentance (hope)."[16]

Much like the definition of shame, the exposure of our sin should distress us as we become conscious of our wrongs. But as the Holman Bible Dictionary explains, our distress should drive us to repentance, turning our despair into hope and healing. Like Newton, we can change from wretch to worshipper of God.

In further studying the difference between shame and guilt, I found an article by Kegan Mosier of Cornerstone Christian Counseling helpful. Kegan says guilt is behavior-focused, and shame is identity-focused. Guilt says, "I did something disgusting," while shame says, "I am disgusting."[17] This definition shows us that guilt and conviction focus on our behavior, which leads us to hope and change. At the same time, shame is identity-focused and leaves us stuck in despair. When we don't fully grasp our identity as redeemed children of our heavenly Father, we will believe the lies of the Enemy and will continue to live in the shame of who we were before our new life in Christ. Or, if we aren't fully living in our redeemed identity, we can be deceived into feeling shame and guilt over things we are not responsible for.

What about you? Are you ready to live as a redeemed child of God and leave your shame and guilt—real or false—at the foot of the cross? Our Savior took our shame and bore it for us so we wouldn't have to.

The Woman at the Well

> *Jesus said to her, "Everyone who drinks of this water will be thirsty again, but whoever drinks of the water that I will give him will never be thirsty again. The water that I will give him will become in him a spring of water welling up to eternal life."* **John 4:13–14**

The Samaritan woman, also known as the woman at the well, is an example of someone who could have easily let shame define her. She lived in the town of Samaria and had come to draw water from Jacob's well. Jesus was passing that way and sat down near the well to rest, as He was weary from His journey. As she approached the well, Jesus asked her to give Him a drink. She was caught off guard that He—a Jewish man—would ask anything from her—a Samaritan woman—or even converse with her. When she inquired why he would ask her for a drink, Jesus turned the conversation from the water in the well, which could only quench her thirst temporarily, to the Living Water that quenches thirst forever.

Once again, we see how the Savior elevates the status of a woman by interacting with her directly in an intimate conversation—a situation unheard of in that culture. Jesus confronted her about her life with truth and grace by asking her questions He already knew the answers to. She'd had five different husbands, and the man she was currently living with was *not* her husband.

Perhaps one of her greatest fears was being alone. The fact that she was drawing water alone at midday indicates she was a social outcast, even among her own people. Likewise, we don't know if the five divorces were all her fault. Men in that society could divorce their wives for less than noble reasons, leaving the woman to bear the shame alone. Either way, Jesus revealed Himself to this woman as the Messiah, the Living Water, who came to quench her thirst for significance and security. She had not found this security in men; she had only found shame. When changed by this interaction with Jesus, we see her become one of Christ's first evangelists as she tells the people of her town, "Come, see a man who told me all that I ever did. Can this be the Christ?" (John 4:29). What an encouragement it is to us to see how this once despised Samaritan woman, who was living what was considered a shameful life, was transformed by the Living Water!

My friend Judy tells the story of how Jesus met her right where she was during a time of deep grief and delivered her from the shame she had been carrying after two failed marriages. Judy (J. C. Lafler) is a prolific fiction writer and her book *Love–What's God Got to Do with It?* is a sweet story about a fitness instructor who meets her future husband when he takes a class she is teaching. Her book is based on how Judy actually met her current husband—the first man to show her unconditional love—and his love led her back to the Living Water! Read here what Judy discovered about finding freedom from shame:

> I always wanted to be a nurse. I worked hard in school and earned a scholarship in nursing. But I got pregnant, married, had two children, gave up the nursing scholarship, and divorced, all within ten years of my high school graduation. I viewed myself as a failure and was ashamed of how my life had turned out.

85

I threw myself into striving to prove myself a good mom, and I reapplied and made it back into the nursing program. I worked hard to provide a good life for my children, but I met another man with three children of his own. We were married soon after meeting, and I tried to handle the increased workload of five children while keeping up with college classes. But I soon realized I couldn't manage it all and once again dropped out of the program.

During a rocky stretch in our marriage, we had a child together, thinking it would unite us. It didn't. My husband was mentally and physically abusive, and after almost a decade together, we divorced. He blamed me for our problems and wounded my heart further by labeling me stupid and announcing he should never have married me. I once again felt ashamed of how my life was turning out.

After months of depression, I returned to college and finished my associate's degree. I started writing again, a passion that had always energized me, and I won a scholarship to a weekend writer's conference. I met with authors and editors and performed a poetry reading. After seasons of loneliness, I had finally found my people. They understood me. They *liked* me. After the encouragement I received about my writing and poetry, I knew I had to find more time to dedicate to it and the people who accepted me.

But the demands of my home and work life were still there. One night, when my kids were out, I sat on the floor in the middle of my living room and finally cried out to God. "Please, God, lead me to what you created me for." I was still feeling deep shame over my two failed marriages. The second marriage had wounded me deeply, and I thought I deserved the pain. I cried and cried as I talked to God, lamenting my sin and failures and begging Him to understand and love me. I could almost *feel* him listening.

After that night, I was excited to get back to praying and going to church. But growing kids meant growing expenses, so I took a second job, working at our local YMCA. I worked in the Nautilus center, where I agreed to teach a spinning class. I knew it was a lot, and I prayed for the strength to excel and prove I was not the failure my ex-husband labeled me.

After almost a year, something amazing happened. A handsome man joined my spinning class one night. He invited me to play racquetball and have dinner. He wanted to spend time with me, and he listened to me. He read my poetry and talked to me about God. When life as a single mother working two jobs got tough, David did something no other man had done for me. He took my hands in his and prayed for me. I began to feel God's presence in a new and fresh way. I began to understand that God was my heavenly Father, and just as He saw and spoke to the Samaritan woman, He was speaking to me. He saw her brokenness and my brokenness, but He was not ashamed of me. He was proud of me and wanted to heal my wounds and redeem my past. My heavenly Father had been pursuing me and waiting patiently for me to turn to Him, trust in His Son Jesus, and believe that Jesus had died on the cross for my sins and carried my shame so I wouldn't have to. Like the Samaritan woman, He showed me the source of Living Water where I would never have to thirst for acceptance or fear being ashamed and alone again.

David and I were married eight months after we met and will soon celebrate our twenty-fifth wedding anniversary! My life has changed dramatically as God's good plan for me has unfolded. I love my times in fellowship with God, as I've learned to trust Him … talk to Him … believe in Him. I enjoy rich times reading His Word daily, and I always thank Him for the gift He gave me in my husband, David.

Hope and a Future

Dear reader, are you struggling with feelings of shame after experiencing abuse or a divorce? Or maybe you're still burdened with guilt over your past mistakes? I urge you to close your eyes and imagine yourself kneeling before your heavenly Father. Can you picture yourself telling Him that the sacrifice of His Son, Jesus Christ, wasn't enough to save you from your shame? This thought is unfathomable! Let's instead bow before Him and express our gratitude for Christ's finished work. Yes, we are great sinners, but

Why Do I Still Feel Shame?

Christ is a great Savior. We can rest in the embrace of our heavenly Father, knowing that we are His beloved children. Jesus died on the cross to take away our shame and guilt, and He doesn't want us to carry those burdens any longer. Let's follow the example of my friend Judy and release our shame, embracing our true identity as children of God. You too, my friend, can find hope and a bright future by believing in Him and letting Him redeem your past. Trust in His love and promise, and you will find significance in His embrace.

A Prayer for His Beloved

Dear heavenly Father, I praise You for Your amazing grace. I pray I will understand the depths of Your love in sending Your Son to save wretched and miserable sinners like John Newton and me. I pray You will show me any areas where I am still living with shame and lead me on the path to healing. Please show me that my past, present, and future sin do not affect my identity as Your daughter. Please help me put my hope and joy in You, our great Savior, and impress on my heart that Your grace is greater than all my sin. Father, like the Samaritan woman, may I drink deeply of the Living Water and never thirst for significance again as I rest in the fact that You bore my shame on the cross so I wouldn't have to. May the beauty of Psalm 34:5 surround me: "Those who look to him are radiant, and their faces shall never be ashamed."

In Jesus's name, amen.

Questions for Reflection

1. Describe a time you felt tormented by thoughts of your sin and mistakes. Have you considered that you may be stuck in shame instead of moving from conviction to hope?

2. Read Ephesians 2:4–6. What do these verses tell you about your significance to God?

3. Do you have children, grandchildren, or other loved ones who are thirsting after the things of the world instead of drinking from the Living Water? Read these words from Isaiah 44:3 and put your hope in Jesus's power to save. "For I will pour water on the thirsty land, and streams on the dry ground; I will pour my Spirit upon your offspring, and my blessing on your descendants."

4. Read Zephaniah 3:19. What does God say He will do for the oppressed, the lame, and the outcast?

5. How do you allow shame from your past to hold you back in ministry? What is a practical step you can take today to move forward?

Chapter Six

Does God See Me?

But you, O Lord, know me; you see me, and test
my heart toward you.

JEREMIAH 12:3

ot again. I collapsed onto the second to the last step of our steep basement stairs. With one hand, I clung to the smooth wooden rail as my arm stretched across the horizontal surface of the risers. The earthy, rotten-egg smell in the room reached my nostrils. Raw sewage had seeped into our lower level once again. Feeling defeated, silent tears fell as my eyes moved to the new carpet that would need to be replaced. I surveyed the wooden boxes now sitting in polluted water. Those plain brown boxes looked inconsequential on the outside, but inside, they held precious memories—unfinished baby books, photo albums, and other keepsakes. The tree roots below the ground surrounding our home had steadily and quietly stretched downward toward the buried sewer line, causing a pipeline to crack.

The problems those tree roots caused are much like the way an iceberg below the surface does great damage to an unsuspecting ship. Like icebergs, tree roots, and our own buried discontentment, sometimes it's not what you see above that's the issue—it's what lies below. If we don't take care of a root of discontentment stealthily wrapping itself around our hearts, toxic waste eventually rises to the surface.

The eight-hundred-square-foot, sixty-year-old Cape Cod home we had purchased in Hammond, Indiana, had lost its initial charm. We had recently endured a robbery, and our camcorder was among the items the thieves made off with. The camcorder could be replaced, but not the tape left inside. It was a video recording of our recent summer vacation with our kids and the special time with their cousins. I wondered if the kids' photo albums, now sitting in dirty water, would also be lost.

My mind drifted to the time soon after the robbery when a young man walking in the alleyway adjacent to our home exposed himself to our eight-year-old daughter, who was innocently playing in our backyard. The relentless tree roots now wreaking havoc on our pipes and causing our basement to flood with stench was the last straw. I was anxious to move and had grown impatient and discontent.

God, do you see me? I cried.

Baby Joseph had awoken me from a deep sleep twice the night before, and I was oh so tired. I also was struggling with muscle weakness, which made climbing the stairs to the children's bedrooms at night more difficult. We had no family in town but were serving in a church where almost everyone was related. It was hard not to envy those who had parents, grandparents, aunts, or siblings to come alongside and help them. I sometimes felt like I was all alone in the wilderness of parenting.

After the robbery and a deterioration of my health, a dear benefactress gifted us with money for a down payment on a new house. This recent widow wanted us to find a home in an area where our kids could safely play—and one without stairs for me to maneuver. The months of house hunting, however, dragged on, and I grew discouraged. Amid the darkness, I had lost hope. I needed to walk by faith and not by sight and to believe the promise of the God who sees me.

Have you ever felt isolated in your suffering? Or felt yourself slipping into the depths of despair and wondering if God was listening to your prayers? Like me, has discontentment or bitterness ever slowly wrapped roots around your unsuspecting heart?

The God Who Sees

> So she called the name of the Lord who spoke to her, "You are a God of seeing," for she said, "Truly here I have seen him who looks after me." **Genesis 16:13**

God had promised Abraham and Sarah a son in their old age, but twenty-five years had passed since that promise, and Sarah was tired of waiting. She decided to remedy the situation herself by giving her Egyptian servant Hagar to Abraham in hopes of having a child through her. As a slave, Hagar was Sarah's property and had no choice in the matter. After she became pregnant by Abraham with a child that would not be hers to keep, Hagar looked at Sarah with contempt. Sarah grew bitter and angry about Hagar's attitude and dealt harshly with her, causing Hagar to run away.

The angel of the Lord found Hagar by a spring of water in the wilderness where she had fled to get away from Sarah's mistreatment. The angel spoke kindly to her, told her to return to her mistress Sarah, and promised to increase her offspring greatly. The angel also told Hagar that God had listened to her affliction and that she would have a son and call him Ishmael.

Despite all that life had thrown at her, Hagar found significance in the God who saw her, heard her affliction, and looked after her. "'You are a God of seeing,' for she said, 'Truly here I have seen him who looks after me'" (Genesis 16:13). God saw Hagar, and Hagar saw God's loving hand.

Walk by Faith, Not by Sight

Hagar's mistress Sarah also found significance in the God who sees. Twenty-five years after Abraham was told that Sarah would conceive, she bore Isaac, the son of promise. But why the twenty-five-year wait? God could have fulfilled His promise the day He spoke it. Jeremiah 12:3 says, "But you, O Lord, know me; you see me, and test my heart toward you." Perhaps God was testing her heart toward Him. Would she believe in the dark what He had promised in the light? Faith is being sure of what we hope for and certain of what we cannot see (Hebrews 11:1). It's not faith if we can see it.

Oftentimes, I relate more to Sarah than Hagar. I was overwhelmed by God's love and provision when He saw me and promised to provide a new home through the generosity of one of His servants. I felt His embrace. Yet I'm embarrassed to admit that six short months after His promise to me, I was growing impatient with God and my husband. Why was it taking Alan so long to find a house we could agree on? I was happy with several of the ones we toured, but he was not. Why was he being so picky? They were all better than where we were currently living. *Let's just pick one!*

That evening with the mess in the basement waiting for us to strip and clean, I pressed to get my way on one of the houses we had viewed. But in the middle of my diatribe, I heard a voice. It wasn't audible, but the words were clear as a bell inside my head.

You're acting like Sarah.

Those four words stopped me in my tracks. I realized I was taking matters into my own hands and pushing my husband to buy a house he didn't feel was right for us. Like Sarah, I had grown impatient waiting on the promise and was going to fix it myself.

Christian author and speaker Elisabeth Elliot says, "Restlessness and impatience change nothing except our peace and joy. Peace does not dwell in outward things, but in the heart prepared to wait trustfully and quietly on him who has all things safely in his hands."[18]

Our impatience doesn't truly fix the problem, but it does rob us of our joy and peace. We will never find lasting contentment in things. Our heart only finds peace when we wait upon God in faith.

He Came to Seek and Rescue

In her impatience and discontentment, Hagar decided to fix the problem of her dire circumstances by running away. She had not yet prayed to God, yet the angel said to her, "The Lord has listened to your affliction."

About that beautiful sentence spoken to Hagar, the famous Baptist preacher Charles Haddon Spurgeon said,

> But thy deep sorrow has cried to him. Thou art oppressed, and the Lord has undertaken for thee. Thou art suffering heavily, and God, the All-pitiful,

has heard thy affliction. Grief has an eloquent voice when mercy is the listener. Woe has a plea which goodness cannot resist. Though sorrow and woe ought to be attended with prayer, yet even when supplication is not offered, the heart of God is moved by misery itself. In Hagar's case, the Lord heard her affliction: he looked forth from his glory upon that lone Egyptian woman who was in the deepest distress in which a woman could well be placed, and he came speedily to her help.[19]

Hagar's deep sorrow cried to God before she knew how to call upon Him herself. The heart of God was moved by her misery before she even uttered a prayer for help. Likewise, before we called upon His name, God sent Jesus to seek and save the lost. Before we knew we were dead, He sent His Son to make us alive.

God Works While We Wait

God was working behind the scenes to provide the perfect home for us while I tried to fix the situation myself. In her article for *Desiring God*, Jade Mazarin says,

> The story of Adam and Eve is a story of rebellion against God. Once they believed that God didn't have their best interests in mind, they decided to go ahead without God and do what they wanted. They became, in effect, their own god. Too often, this is exactly what we do today. When God tells us to wait, we don't trust

him, but go ahead and find ways to accomplish what
we want to happen.[20]

Like Adam and Eve, when we don't trust that God is working
out the details in our lives for our good, we lose faith and rebel. We
move ahead to find our own way to accomplish what we want.

Shortly after the clear rebuke from the Holy Spirit about acting
like Sarah, I quit trying to fix things on my own ... and then God
showed up and showed off. My husband found a precious home for
our family. It was for sale by owner, the couple not using a realtor
because the homes in that sought-after location were selling within a
couple of weeks of going on the market. As soon as it was listed, their
phone started ringing.

This sweet Christian couple prayed that someone would buy
their beloved home who would care for it as much as they did. But on
the third day of the listing, the calls stopped coming. Their phone fell
silent, not even ringing with news from a couple who had been quite
interested in the house with intentions to call back about seeing it
again that day. The mystery was solved, however, when they realized
the phone was not put back on the receiver all the way. As soon as the
wife corrected that, the phone rang—my husband wanting to come
by and see the home.

They said he could come right then, which he did, and they
talked for over an hour while he toured their lovely home—a one-
story, spacious ranch with the master and kids' bedrooms all on one
floor. My husband was able to take me back with the kids to see
it that same evening. We all loved it as much as he did and knew
this home would be a tremendous blessing for us. When the other

interested couple finally communicated with the sellers, the owners told them it was sold. They felt God wanted us to have it even though the other couple was willing to pay more.

God saw me in the wilderness of suffering, and He provided beautifully for our family. But He was calling me to walk by faith and not by sight (2 Corinthians 5:7). Your suffering may look very different from mine, dear reader, but He sees you too. You may feel forgotten by others, but you are significant to God. Let's heed the exhortation of Elisabeth Elliott: "Don't dig up in doubt what you planted in faith."[21]

My friend Missy Linkletter tells the story of how God saw her grief and suffering, and even before her prayers were offered, the heart of God saw her affliction and sent her help. Hear from her about finding significance in the God who sees:

> I was not a well-liked child. Often the new student, I tried to reinvent myself with the hope of making just one friend. But kids could sense weakness, and I radiated insecurity. I envied the girls with the creamy complexions—my face covered with freckles in a pattern that resembled the Milky Way. My school desk was always a mess, and I was easily distracted. I tried with all my might to focus, but I struggled to quiet the chaos that hummed through my mind. The teacher didn't know what to do with me. Her solution, it seemed, was to move my desk to the farthest corner of the room. It was humiliating.
>
> My home life felt even more unbearable. We'd moved plenty of times, and now were at it again. I received

no warning when we were evicted from the rental house. I was picked up from school, and instead of going home, we went to a run-down motel. Old dingy drapes hung from the window, one small round table sat in the corner, and two queen beds completed the rest of the room. This little room would house our family of five for months to come.

I remembered how a smoky haze filled the air, and the noise of the television blaring made it nearly impossible for my already crowded brain to string two thoughts together. I craved privacy and eventually created my own space by draping a blanket over the small round table. There I would sit and enjoy my slice of solitude.

Later, as the day drew to a close, dread began to increase. With much alcohol flowing, the night reached its fever pitch as my dad became combative and belligerent. Somehow I was supposed to fall asleep while my parents fought into the wee hours of the morning. When morning dawned, and it was time for me to get up and be driven to school, they often refused to wake up, making me tardy or altogether absent. This, of course, affected my already poor performance, and my teacher disapproved of me all the more.

I spent a lot of time in the motel swimming pool. The summer before, I had been a part of the swim team at the public pool, competing in the breaststroke. I loved being part of a team. So, with great anticipation, I went down to the motel pool each day after school and swam. With each lap, I took great care, paying particular attention to my form. Because, after all, anything could happen. Maybe an Olympic scout would show up at our little motel, see me swimming, and recruit me to train for the Olympics!

As school drew to a close and summer arrived, we had an unexpected visitor. It was our old neighbor from the rental house. He and his wife had hosted vacation Bible school in their home the summer before. The lemonade and cookies had wooed me. Somehow, he found us at the motel to ask if I could join his family for summer camp. I could hardly believe my ears. *What? He came to find me?* You can imagine my shock when my parents agreed to let me attend.

That next week, I boarded a big white bus with a lot of kids I'd never met and drove to my first Christian summer camp. Bible stories, songs, and arts and crafts filled our days. I loved every moment. When it was time to come back home, I walked away with a certificate for camper of the week, but more importantly, with seeds of the gospel planted in my heart.

Five years later, a friend invited me to go to church, and I couldn't think of anything that sounded more boring ... until she told me about a bunch of cute boys who were there. That was enough to get me in the door. Much to my surprise, I loved it at church. The people were so kind, and it was the most peaceful place I'd ever experienced. I became a faithful attender, and several months later, the pastor shared the gospel with me. I prayed with him that night, surrendering my heart to Jesus Christ. I was filled with hope, excitement, and, most of all, peace.

The circumstances in my home life became increasingly more complex, and I would remain there for several more years. But God was with me, and He changed me. He took my heart of stone and replaced it with a heart of flesh (Ezekiel 36:26).

The Olympic scout never showed up, but the God who sees called me by name. He rescued me, and I stand secure in Him. My desk no longer sits in the corner. Instead, I have the privilege of sharing the healing found in Jesus Christ with many women who have been broken just like me.

Finding Significance in God's Embrace

Have you experienced God's personal love that seeks us before we seek Him, the way Hagar and my friend Missy have? Regarding Hagar's experience of transitioning from knowing about God to knowing Him as the God who sees, Spurgeon said,

> None doubt the existence of God when God has come into contact with their spirit. When we have felt his power and tasted his love, and known his overwhelming influence, then have we said, "Jehovah, he is the God," and we have bowed in solemn worship

before him. I do not know that Hagar had ever thought of God before; but she discerns him now and speaks wisely. No doubt she had heard of Jehovah, for she had joined in the devotions of Abraham's family; but now for the first time in her life she recognizes in deed and of a truth that the Lord lives for her, and therefore she speaks to him, and calls him, "The God that sees."[22]

Even those who have questioned the existence of God no longer doubt when He touches their spirit. When they feel His power and taste His love, they bow in worship, and like Hagar, proclaim Him as the God who sees.

Like my friend Missy, have you found your significance in His pursuing love? If so, I invite you to rest securely in His embrace.

A Prayer for His Beloved

Dear heavenly Father, I praise You as *El Roi,* the God who sees us. We are never left alone in our suffering, and there is no place Your children can flee from Your presence. I pray I will understand that while I am waiting, You are working. I pray You will show me any areas where I am trying to fix things on my own, instead of waiting upon You. Like Hagar, may I call upon the name of the Lord who spoke to her, and, likewise, may my heart declare, "You are a God of seeing. Truly here I have seen him who looks after me." In Jesus's name, amen.

Questions for Reflection

1. Describe a time you felt unseen and alone.
2. Read Jeremiah 12:3. What three things do you learn about God's care for you?
3. Read Genesis 16:13. What name did Hagar use for God? How does this name/attribute of God bring comfort to your heart?
4. Describe a time you tried to dig up in doubt something you planted in faith.
5. What is a practical step you can take today to relinquish control of a difficult circumstance or person? How can you walk by faith and not by sight? Remember, while you are waiting, God is working!

Chapter Seven

How Do I Release My Adult Children?

By faith Moses, when he was born, was hidden
for three months by his parents, because they saw
that the child was beautiful, and they were
not afraid of the king's edict.

HEBREWS 11:23

"I want my epidural, please and thank you!" Those were some of the first words out of my mouth after being wheeled into the labor and delivery ward of the hospital. I was there for the birth of our second child, so this was not my first rodeo.

I learned a few things from my experience of giving birth to our daughter, Hannah, just nineteen months prior. Although when I arrived at the hospital for her delivery, I was resolute that I was going the all-natural route. My husband and I attended the Lamaze classes, where I learned all the proper breathing techniques. During my first birthing experience, however, my initial determination dissolved during my twenty-third hour of labor. A nurse caught me in a weak moment while writhing in pain, and I agreed to an epidural. Then, shortly after the anesthesia took effect, I thought, *Why didn't I let them give me this lovely medicine twenty-three hours ago?*

So with this second birth, I asked immediately, and the anesthesiologist arrived with the medicine soon after. The drug worked its magic, and my husband and I were joking with the nurses about something when the energy in the room abruptly changed. We had been in labor and delivery for just over two hours when the vibe in the room transformed from joyful expectation to looks of grave concern on the faces of my caretakers. As everyone began anxiously fluttering about, a nurse turned the baby's heart monitor around so I could no longer view it. Then a nurse quickly placed an oxygen mask over my nose and mouth. Again, this was not my first rodeo, so I immediately recognized these actions as very different from those during our first daughter's birth. There were obviously complications with the delivery of baby number two, but no one was telling me what they were.

The initial excitement of this second birth transitioned to an anxious feeling in the pit of my swollen, pregnant belly, and then panic began to slowly rise. When I tried to ask questions about what was happening, the nurse told me I needed to keep the thick plastic oxygen mask over my mouth. She assured me that the doctor was on his way and would answer our questions. However, fear gripped my heart tighter when I realized my husband had left my side. My eyes anxiously darted about the room until I noticed him with another nurse in the doorway. She spoke to him in hushed tones. Then as my nostrils filled with the smell of antiseptic and alcohol, anxious nausea in the pit of my stomach rose to my throat.

Thankfully, the doctor appeared just in time, and his calm demeanor eased my nausea and panic. My body then seemed to transition instantaneously into hard labor, and it was time for me to start the pushing phase of delivery. I was in labor for only four hours total, from start to finish, when our son Daniel entered this world. But unlike Hannah's lily-white appearance, Daniel was completely blue.

Our newborn son arrived in the hospital delivery room the same color as *Aladdin*'s genie. The umbilical cord had not only wrapped around his neck but, more seriously, contained a knot. The nurse who turned the baby monitor had seen our son's heartbeat going in and out, indicating an issue. If his delivery had lasted much longer, the situation would have been much graver.

When Daniel's lungs inflated with air shortly after his arrival, I felt the room breathe a collective sigh of relief.

As a sense of calm returned to the atmosphere, the OB-GYN and staff kept saying what a lucky baby Daniel was. My husband and I kept changing the word *lucky* to *blessed*. The doctor also told us that he had previously delivered a stillborn with the same type of knot in his umbilical cord as Daniel's. He explained that during a long delivery, as the cord is stretched, it cuts off the oxygen supply to the baby. I felt lightheaded again as he described how Daniel's birth could have ended in death, but I was then filled with a strong sense of *knowing*. I knew the events surrounding our baby's birth were not about luck, but about God. My Lord had preserved Daniel's life for a purpose. I thought of Mary, the mother of Jesus, as I pondered these things in my heart.

We went on to have two more children, first another girl and then another boy, to complete our family of six. When Daniel was two years old, I had another knowing feeling while doing my daily Bible reading. As I read Luke 22:31–32, I felt the Holy Spirit impress something upon my heart regarding Daniel's life. These are not typical life verses a mother would choose for her child, but they began to invade my mind during my prayer time amid difficult seasons with our son time and again. I believe these verses were selected for Daniel from God above. Likewise, they brought me hope during seasons of soul-wounding grief over our oldest son.

The first verse was like a sword thrust, piercing my heart, as it was a picture of the battles Daniel would face: "Simon, Simon, behold, Satan demanded to have you, that he might sift you like wheat" (Luke 22:31). The second verse, however, gave me comforting hope and strength to persevere in prayer amid seasons of warfare. It is a *but God* verse that sheds light on the darkness of the journey with a prodigal son. It is a promise our Savior spoke to Peter after first issuing the warning that Satan desired to have him. "But I have prayed for you that your faith may not fail. And when you have turned again, strengthen your brothers." During seasons when I felt my heart would break open, I clung to the hope of Christ's intercession for our son.

Later, my husband and I would learn that Daniel's birth experience was only the first of numerous times this child would cheat death. From serious accidents, totaled cars, lightning strikes within a foot of where he had been standing, and many other near misses, Daniel seemed to have nine lives as he grew to adulthood. Yet amid our fears and tears, and despite the Enemy's attacks, God was at work in Daniel's life behind the scenes. However, like Jochebed, Moses's mother, I would have to learn to release him to the Lord.

How Do I Release My Adult Children?

A Fine Child

> *Now a man from the house of Levi went and took as his wife a Levite woman. The woman conceived and bore a son, and when she saw that he was a fine child, she hid him three months. When she could hide him no longer, she took for him a basket made of bulrushes and daubed it with bitumen and pitch.* **Exodus 2:1–3**

As we discussed in a previous chapter, Scripture tells us about a unique child who was born during a horrific genocide. The evil Pharoah had instructed that all newborn male Israelites be killed. Yet we read that Jochebed saw her son, Moses, as a fine child. She recognized the calling on his life from God. So she hid him and then placed him in a basket by the river, where he was found and adopted by Pharoah's daughter.

Anie Trimmer, in a Mother's Day article for the women's ministry of the Salvation Army, says the following about Jochebed:

> Because Jochebed trusts and fears Him, God gives this mother the courage and ability to think clearly and creatively, thereby fulfilling God's redemptive plan for Moses and the entire nation. However, saving her son's life comes with a cost. Though she is blessed to nurse and nurture him for a short time, she must be willing to relinquish her son to be adopted and raised by someone else. This is a mother's love, making great sacrifices and being willing to do the difficult things that parenting requires. As God quietly orchestrates

events in the life of Jochebed, be assured that He is working behind the scenes in your life as well.[23]

Parenting requires great wisdom and great sacrifice. When God calls us to release our children, we must relinquish control. Just as God was working behind the scenes in the lives of Moses and Jochebed, we must have faith that He is also working behind the scenes in our children's lives as well.

It took tremendous courage for Jochebed to hide Moses from the Egyptians and great faith to release him to the Lord. I wonder if she thought she must have misheard God about the calling on his life when, years later, Moses committed murder and then fled into the wilderness. Did she feel bewildered and hopeless when it seemed Moses was not the promised deliverer to rescue her people from slavery? Did she take the guilt of his actions upon herself?

We know the story does not end with Moses running away. As we continue reading in Exodus, we see Moses experienced a miraculous call from God and did indeed lead the Israelites out of Egypt. Likewise, we need to remember that just as Jochebed could not bear responsibility for her son murdering an Egyptian and fleeing into the wilderness, nor could she take credit for his being raised up by God to lead the children of Israel out of Egypt.

Releasing Responsibility

With all four of our kids, I can honestly say that I made great sacrifices. Yet, sadly, I feel I fell quite short when it came to exercising wisdom. I did not begin working through the pain of my past until my early forties. Unfortunately, people-pleasing and being controlled by other people's opinions affected my parenting. I now realize that when we operate and parent from a place of hurt rather than from a place of healing, we miss things. I missed Daniel's anxiety struggles. I missed his attention deficit disorder. I missed the abuse he endured as a child. There is so, so much I would change and do differently. But my heavenly Father has shown me that operating from a place of guilt and shame is not what He wants for me—or for any us.

We must trust that He is faithful to forgive us when we confess our sins, and He expects us to also forgive ourselves. Like Jochebed, we should not take too much credit for what our kids do right, and we aren't to take too much blame for what they do wrong. And when the Enemy tells us we've ruined our offspring because of our sins and mistakes, remember we are not that powerful.

God at Work Behind the Scenes

"Daniel, this is not about you. It's about your dad's parenting." A misguided youth director spoke these words to our son—a man Daniel considered a friend when he was still a teenager. This youth director had gone back several years on Daniel's social media profile, took meticulous notes, and built a case against him to prove that Daniel was a rebellious youth. I believe his main goal, however, was to prove that Daniel's father, my husband, was unfit for pastoral ministry. Learning that someone in the church had painstakingly spent numerous hours researching examples to illustrate ways in which my son was not acting like a Christian, only to say it was not about him, was a sword thrust into my heart. It was clear to me that this youth director's primary concern was not the soul of my son but, instead, having my husband removed from his pastoral position.

I realize I am writing about something that happened many years ago and only from my perspective. Some other people involved have quite a different view. But what is important is that I am called to process the pain, forgive—which means release him and his offense to God—and move forward.

Shortly after this time of trauma and un-Christlike responses from all sides, Daniel gave up on the church and fell deeper into the pit of self-medication. Finally, my husband and I had to release him and withdraw our help. This led to a painful separation that words can't describe. I began to imagine the anguish Jochebed must have experienced when Moses fled into the wilderness and she lost contact.

While that is Daniel's story to tell, I will say I can now look back with joy at how God worked things out in our son's life. It is a delight to see our precious son returning to his faith and thriving in his career and conduct. God is restoring the years the locusts have eaten and rebuilding our family from the bottom up. The Lord had to show my husband and me that this was not just about our boy but also about the plowing and refining needed in our own hearts.

Friend, if you are currently in a wilderness season with a prodigal who seems to be running far from the Father's arms, I encourage you to remember that God is at work behind the scenes. As you pray for your child's return to the fold, lean into what God is doing in your own heart. Also remember that motherhood is an important role, a high and holy calling, yet it's not where we find our significance. Placing our significance in our role as parent instead of our identity in Christ leads to devastation if one of our children chooses a direction we don't like. Pride and joy in our kids can easily lead to bitterness toward them when they disappoint us. But when our identity is in Christ, our significance and security is assured in the shelter of our heavenly Father's embrace.

Like Jochebed, we are called to walk by faith, not by sight. Her faith was so strong that she and her husband are mentioned in God's hall of the faithful in Hebrews 11:23. Walking by faith, we don't need to fear our soul's enemy or man's plans against our children. Instead, let's hide our children in the covering of prayer and release them to the heavenly Father's care.

My friend Christine Trimpe tells the story of fighting for her son in court and with the medical community after he suffered a traumatic brain injury. She also shares the journey of learning to relinquish responsibility for missteps in the aftermath of the accident. Like Jochebed, she had to learn to release her son by faith into God's care. Amid the trauma—and during the confusion and weariness of 2020—Christine found relentless joy through her time in God's Word, and God led her to write an Advent devotional on the Gospel of Luke. In her book *Seeking Joy through the Gospel of Luke: A Christmas to Calvary Advent Countdown,* Christine writes, "Even during times of uncertainty and major changes, the joy of the Lord sustains those who know Him and spend time in His Word."[24] We can all learn from this courageous mother:

> At twenty-three, my son Kyle had been rear-ended at a standstill in traffic at 70 mph by a distracted driver. There was no airbag to protect him, and the impact knocked him out cold. The doctors took no medical history in the trauma emergency department that day, and they never mentioned the possibility of the devastating effects on mental health due to a closed head injury with loss of consciousness, especially in a

susceptible individual.

Kyle was a susceptible individual, though I wasn't even aware of that until reading a doctor's diagnosis months after searching for answers to Kyle's new personality and bizarre behavior. The doctor's words in his neuropsychological report pierced my heart but set me on a path of turning this season of sorrow over to the Lord. *Based on the mother's description of her induced labor (with the aid of a vacuum extractor during birth), I cannot rule out the possibility that he may have sustained an unsuspected prenatal or perinatal birth trauma. If so, it would have made him much more vulnerable to the subsequent head trauma and cerebral jarring he experienced in connection with his 2017 automobile accident.*

When Kyle's behavior changes began to emerge after the accident, I never attributed any of it to the loss of consciousness and resulting traumatic brain injury. And so, like Cheryl, I berated myself daily for my failures in protecting and understanding my son. I found myself being angry with Kyle for his behavior, which I now know was beyond his control. It took us two full years to find a healthcare provider who put the puzzle pieces together. Several neuropsychologists agreed on a mood disorder diagnosis due to traumatic brain injury.

Before the diagnosis, I lamented with the Lord: *What did I do wrong in his upbringing to bring about this unusual and frequently scary behavior?* And after his diagnosis, I still found a way to blame myself. *How could I have missed this? Why did I not know closed head injury could result in these changes?*

Learning that Kyle may have been much more susceptible to other effects of brain injury due to birth trauma helped me see that every part of this post-accident life was most certainly out of my control. I was grateful when one compassionate doctor took the time to look me in the eyes and explain Kyle's situation, helping me release much of the burden of blaming myself for missing all the signs and symptoms. So while early intervention is vital with brain injury, and we had missed out on two years of early care, God allowed me to release myself and feel grateful we were finally on the right path to getting Kyle the proper treatment.

I could fill pages with details of our trials and tribulations over the past five years. We had to go through a real-life trial in a court of law, fighting a gigantic billion-dollar insurance company, to seek justice for Kyle's injuries. They didn't believe a word of our harrowing story. And they still don't believe or understand the years of loss we have suffered.

In the Lord's sovereign mercy, He led me on my own healing journey a mere six months before Kyle's accident. He healed me physically, emotionally, and spiritually. During this time, God wooed me into His

Word every morning, and it was my source of comfort and strength during the difficult season of many unanswered questions about Kyle. As I cried out to the Lord every day to heal my son, God miraculously increased my joy and my faith and grew my confidence and trust in His promises.

The most impactful lessons I learned:

- You can carry joy and sorrow simultaneously.
- Our job is to trust God. God's job is the outcome.
- God cares about our children more than we will ever comprehend.

I learned to surrender my anxiety and worries regarding Kyle's future to the Lord. I've also found an excellent prayer partner in Cheryl. We both have a heart and understanding for young men like Daniel and Kyle. From constant anxiety and worry, I've switched to continuous praise and worship for the young lives God is molding and shaping through these trials. Daniel and Kyle's stories will reflect God's glory in leading others to Him.

The incredible blessing since Kyle's accident is his newfound passion for God's Word. He had never read his Bible before the accident. But God! Now Kyle reads Scripture daily, and we enjoy many conversations about how the Lord works through these storms. Most days we see the sunshine through some scattered clouds.

Just recently, I had to sign a release in our pursuit of justice for Kyle—something painful I didn't want to do but knew the Lord would see us through by His justice and righteousness. The Lord comforted my heart with these beautiful words of David in Psalm 126:5 (NIV, emphasis mine): "Those who sow in tears will reap with *songs of joy*." Jochebed's fight to protect her precious son Moses by hiding him and then placing him by the river must have been sewn in tears. Yet, ultimately, we see in Scripture that her releasing him bore *songs of joy*.

Surely the Lord will also restore these years of loss in our lives. Kyle and I are eager to see what more He will do. Aside from Kyle's new love for God's Word, he also picked up the guitar as a new passion and began playing like someone with years of experience. So I sing those songs of joy as Kyle strums his guitar. It's a beautiful song of joy.

A Prayer for His Beloved

Dear heavenly Father, I praise You for Your everlasting, redeeming love. A love from eternity past to save a people for Yourself. I thank You for the promises found in Galatians 1:3: "Grace to you and peace from God our Father and the Lord Jesus Christ, who gave Himself for our sins to deliver us from the present evil age, according to the will of our God and Father, to whom be the glory forever and ever." I thank You for Your call on Moses's life to deliver Your people from the evils of the land of Egypt. I thank You for giving Jochebed the faith to release Moses to You. Please help me to put my hope in Your sovereign grace and not in the one in my life who has strayed. Please give me peace, comfort, and joy amid my sorrow as I release my loved ones into Your hands. In Jesus's name, amen.

Questions for Reflection

1. Describe a time you felt helpless when someone you loved wandered from the fold of God.
2. Read Hebrews 11:23. Is there someone in your life God is calling you to release control over? How can you replace your fear with faith in God?
3. Read Philippians 1:6. How does this verse bring you comfort?
4. Read John 13:7. Describe a time you didn't understand what was happening in your life until God later revealed the good He had been working behind the scenes.
5. What practical step can you take today to relinquish control of a person you've been desperately trying to rescue or change? How can you walk by faith and not by sight? Remember, while you are waiting, God is working!

Chapter Eight

Where Is My Significance Found?

For I know the plans I have for you, declares the
Lord, plans for welfare and not for evil, to give
you a future and a hope.

JEREMIAH 29:11

I willed my knees to stop shaking as I stepped onto the church platform with my three sisters. I could not control the burning of my cheeks or the echo of my heart pounding in my ears. But as the accompanist began playing "Amazing Grace," the rich and resonating sounds of the piano keys began to distract my nerves. Thankfully, after a glance at my sister Sharyn for courage, the four of us started singing on cue. The hymn was familiar to me and had been one of my mother's favorites, but I had never sung publicly before (and never have since). My sisters and I had agreed to do so that Saturday morning in November as a tribute to my mother at her funeral.

I was twenty-one years old, and my mother's untimely deterioration and death from cancer at fifty had rocked my world, drawing me out of a period of rebellion that began at age fifteen. God captured my heart and returned me to my faith as I faced my mother's mortality. Yet as I stood on that platform singing the gospel's good news, a cloak of shame and unworthiness threatened to overwhelm me. As we sang, however, the Holy Spirit spoke to my heart. He reminded me how amazing God's grace truly is.

> Amazing grace! how sweet the sound
> That saved a wretch like me!
> I once was lost, but now I'm found;
> Was blind, but now I see.[25]

The power of the gospel to redeem and restore indeed began as a sweet sound in my ears and attempted to make its way to my heart. My sisters and I made it through the hymn that day without our emotions overtaking us. Later, our fellow mourners expressed how our offering to our mother also comforted them. Then as the days passed and we all began living our new normal without Mama, joy collided with my sorrow. Remember the single, young pastor named Alan whom I wrote about in another chapter, whom I ended up marrying after returning to Christ? He performed my mom's funeral, and eight months later, we were married in that same church where my sisters and I sang about God's marvelous grace!

I took on the identity of *pastor's wife* as a twenty-two-year-old timid girl, overwhelmed by social anxiety and insecure in the social graces. I wrestled with living in the amazing grace I had sung about, while self-condemning thoughts of my past continued to taunt me.

Thinking back on this time reminds me again of Mary Magdalene. The same power that delivered Mary from seven demons and made her a disciple of Christ also lived in me. The same amazing grace that invited her to travel with Christ, sharing in the ministry and helping provide for His physical needs, was also at work in my life.

The Preacher's Wife

As his first assignment out of seminary at twenty-nine years of age, my soon-to-be husband Alan began serving as an intern and assistant to the senior pastor at a church in Corpus Christi, Texas. A year and a half later, the senior pastor took another call and moved to a different city. Alan was a gifted preacher and teacher, so the church voted to make him their senior pastor. Transitioning from young and single assistant pastor to senior pastor involved a steep learning curve. In addition, since his predecessor had been well-known, seasoned, and beloved by the congregation, the transition was also difficult for the staff and congregation.

Shortly after taking on the senior pastor role, Alan and I met and developed a friendship before marrying the following year. We had two children over the next two and a half years, and ministry demands pressed upon us. Yet the church family showed us much love, grace, and generosity. When Alan resigned three years after we were married to pursue further study and mission work, they surprised us with a generous severance package. We are still close to many of those dear people. It is a special joy when we get to visit the church when we are in town to see my family.

After a year at Covenant Seminary in St. Louis, we took a call in Cape Girardeau, Missouri, where Alan served as the interim pastor while the church searched for a full-time pastor. While in Missouri, our third child—Abigail Emily—was born, which meant we were balancing three kids under four years old! That precious country church in Cape Girardeau provided for our needs and loved us well. We are still in touch with some of those dear people almost thirty years later. That year was one of refreshment before Alan accepted his next call to be the senior pastor of a church in Hammond, Indiana.

We spent eight years serving our church family in that steel town in the northwest part of the state. Our fourth child, Joey, was born there. The congregation was older, and we found ourselves with many surrogate mothers, fathers, grandmothers, and grandfathers. There are always highs and lows in any ministry assignment, but our mutual love for one another in that body of Christ grew deep. Many of those dear saints have gone on to glory now, including my precious spiritual mother from that congregation. But we enjoy keeping in contact with several of those dear saints who are still living.

In 2002, we felt a strong call from God for Alan to accept a position as senior pastor at a church in northwest Georgia. We served that congregation for nine years, and some of my closest friends to this day are ones I initially met in that church. Also, we have much gratitude for the way that body rallied around us during the early days of my health struggles. Yet this assignment ended in a grievous way, as I explained the trauma we went through with our older son in another chapter. Our parenting was called into question, and we experienced our first-ever church split, an indescribably painful season. The soul-wounding sorrow left many bloody, bruised, and searching for answers. The split felt like an ugly divorce, with opposing sides fighting over custody of the children. There was much pain on both sides, but none of our hurt compares to our Lord's. I think of the old hymn, "The Church's One Foundation," by Samuel John Stone.

Tho' with a scornful wonder
the world sees her oppressed,
By schisms rent asunder,
By heresies distressed,
Yet saints their watch are keeping;
Their cry goes up, "How long?"
And soon the night of weeping
Shall be the morn of song.[26]

Yes, our heavenly Father grieves to see His precious bride rent asunder with schisms, breaks, and divisions. But what a glorious promise that the night of weeping will soon be replaced with a morning song! Jesus promises us in Matthew 16:18, "I will build my church, and the gates of hell shall not prevail against it." What a comfort to know that neither our sins nor the sins of others can stop Christ's church from marching forward.

After the gut-wrenching split, the group that left began a new church plant and soon called Alan to be their pastor. For three years, Alan served as their shepherd, and I served in women's and children's ministry—not realizing the wounds from our previous experience had been buried alive. We weren't operating and ministering from a place of healing and realized we just needed some time to recover. Longing for a fresh start in new surroundings and learning that some of our family members in Georgia planned to relocate to the Tampa Bay area of Florida, we decided to move there, thinking that area would become the new family hub. After selling most of our possessions, we loaded up a U-Haul with our dog and youngest son, Joey, our one remaining child still in high school.

Moving to the beach was an exciting adventure. For the first time in our marriage, however, we suddenly had no church family. When we moved from Texas to Missouri, Missouri to Indiana, and Indiana to Georgia, we relocated to meet our new covenant community. But there was no welcome committee when we arrived in Florida, and we felt lost. Until then, our whole married life revolved around the body we were called to serve. Without a church family, we didn't know where to turn. I also began to realize I had been finding significance in my role as a pastor's wife. When that role was stripped away, I felt like a failure.

I initially thought the move to Florida was to trade my role as a pastor's wife for a shiny, new purpose. I believed Florida would be where I finally wrote the book God was calling me to write while Alan developed cross-cultural mission work. However, several months into the move, plans of being a published author and inspirational speaker seemed like a pipe dream.

Several setbacks left us confused and discouraged. The housing we thought we had secured fell through, and we ended up back in apartment living. We also had not been able to raise enough financial support for full-time mission work as we'd hoped. Eventually, Alan found employment teaching in a Christian school, and I began teaching prekindergarten in a private, secular school. I love working with children, but the full-time stress and noise of the classroom were hard on my autoimmune brain. And standing in the hot Florida sun for playground duty sent my body into a relapse. I became increasingly unable to perform my job, forcing me to resign.

Nothing in my life looked like what I thought it should. I felt like I was sitting outside the tomb weeping, without significance or purpose.

Where Is My Significance Found?

Woman, Why Are You Weeping?

> But Mary stood weeping outside the tomb, and
> as she wept she stooped to look into the tomb.
> **John 20:11**

Mary Magdalene, the delivered and transformed traveling disciple of Christ, is now in the depths of despair. We find her bitterly weeping at Jesus's tomb after the crucifixion. It seemed that all was lost. Her beautiful Lord, who had given her purpose in life, was dead. Did this mean she had lost her place in ministry? While navigating the unimaginable loss of her Redeemer and friend, would she have to reinvent herself? In her grief, did she once again find herself searching for significance? Whatever questions she had were soon answered by the appearance of her Savior. We read the beautiful narrative in John 20:15–20:

> Jesus said to her, "Woman, why are you weeping? Whom are you seeking?" Supposing him to be the gardener, she said to him, "Sir, if you have carried him away, tell me where you have laid him, and I will take him away." Jesus said to her, "Mary." She turned and said to him in Aramaic, "Rabboni!" (which means Teacher). Jesus said to her, "Do not cling to me, for I have not yet ascended to the Father; but go to my brothers and say to them, 'I am ascending to my Father and your Father, to my God and your God.'"

Did you notice what caused Mary to recognize Jesus finally? It was when He said her name. This moment reminds me of when I was five months pregnant with our fourth child. We were staying in a large old home on my husband's family property in upstate New York. I had gotten up to use the restroom in the middle of the night while still half asleep. It was our first night there, and I was in unfamiliar surroundings. The long hallway was pitch black, and I walked straight ahead instead of turning back toward the bedroom when exiting the bathroom. What happened next caused my eyes to spring wide open and my heart to skip a beat. It was only one word, but I heard it clearly, almost like an echo. Not an angry tone, but a concerned one. "Cheryl!" At that moment, I looked down, and I was standing at the edge of the landing of an old, steep, wooden staircase. As I stepped backward, my arm instinctively wrapped itself around my swollen, pregnant belly. Through the calling of my name, my baby and I were kept safe. I can only imagine the voice I heard was an angelic being sent by my heavenly Father. It is an experience I will never forget.

How much more miraculous it must have been for Mary. Jesus, back from the dead, live and in person, called her by name! Her Savior showed Mary significance and worth by appearing to her first after His resurrection. He clarified her precious identity as God's daughter when He said He was ascending to His Father and her Father, His God and her God. Though He would leave again, Mary's purpose as Christ's disciple would remain.

The Preacher's Wife, Part Two

Before Florida was on our radar, a retired pastor moved from the Tampa Bay area into our Georgia neighborhood. His name was Phil, and he had come to begin a new ministry to area pastors. Alan and Phil met and became fast friends, and Phil tremendously encouraged Alan when we were navigating the church split. A few years later, we found ourselves in the Sunshine State that Phil had left. Little did we know that God would again use Phil about a year after our move.

Shortly after I had to resign from my job at the pre-K, Alan received a call from Phil, who relayed that the pastor who had replaced him in Florida had decided to pursue another call. Phil's old congregation was about thirty minutes from where we were living, so he asked Alan if he would consider doing some pulpit supply, which meant filling the pulpit on a regular basis while the church searched for a new pastor. What began as supply preaching soon became a full-time position for Alan as senior pastor. His time pastoring this body of Christ would end up being short but very fruitful. We were used by God to encourage and stabilize the church, preparing the way for their next pastor. My husband was able to end his pastoral ministry in a lovely, positive way. Likewise, in my last role as pastor's wife, I started a ladies' Bible study and got a women's ministry off the ground which is still going strong today. God, once again, restored the years the locusts had eaten.

Friend, when we moved to Florida, we had no plans to return to pastoral ministry. But God! He opened the door so miraculously that we joyfully walked through it. While we were stumbling in the wilderness, feeling lonely and lost, God's hand was still upon us. Know that He is also with you, working in extraordinary ways behind the scenes. Remember, whatever your circumstances, you have significance and security in your heavenly Father's embrace. As with Mary Magdalene, He knows His plans for you. They are plans for your welfare and not for evil, to give you a hope-filled future.

My friend Shelly Brown shares her harrowing journey as a neglected, abused, and abandoned orphan and tells of how her heavenly Father showed her that she is His chosen, cherished, and beloved daughter:

> Like Mary Magdalene, I stood bitterly weeping, scared, and devastated by death. However, I was still a child, standing on my tiptoes, peering into the casket where my mama lay. Tears poured down my cheeks, and I gently caressed her cold, porcelain-like hands, quietly begging her to wake up.
>
> As the funeral service started, my dad scooped up my brother and me and sat us on his knees. Then the service seemed to end as quickly as it began. While the adults milled around the small, crowded chapel, I hurriedly made my way back to my mom. I expected that at any moment, she would open her eyes and reach out her arms to me. My little mind couldn't grasp the finality of death, and I certainly could not have imagined what lay ahead of me.
>
> The chapel began to empty, leaving behind only my dad, siblings, and aunts. My dad kissed my brother and me on our cheeks and said goodbye. We didn't know that would be the last time we'd ever see him.
>
> For as long as I could remember, my dad had been in and out of our house after being gone on his drunken binges. He was in no position to care for us and would eventually sign away his parental rights.

"Kids, get in my car. You're going to stay at Sue and Gerry's until we figure things out."

Sue and Gerry were my adult cousins. With three children of their own, the burden we brought into their home, a single-wide trailer, caused a strain and responsibility they were unprepared for.

Instead of gentle arms and tender words of comfort, my questions and cries for my mom were met with, "Stop crying, Shelly, or else I'll give you something to really cry about!"

I quickly discovered that they meant it.

By day my tears dried up, but there was something about the nighttime. As I laid my head on my pillow, alone in the dark, fear and sadness overwhelmed me. *I need my mommy!* Night after night, I cried these words into my pillow so that no one could hear me.

"Mommy, I need you!"

"Can you hear me, Mommy?"

"Please come back and get me!"

"Mommy, please!"

She never came back.

After three months with my cousins, the decision was made to place us in foster care and put us up for adoption. My brother and I would remain together while our sisters were sent to other homes. There was no fanfare or tears in our departure. Just a simple introduction:

"This is Mrs. Goings. She's taking you to your new home, so go get your bags."

My brother and I both had a small plastic bag that carried our few belongings. With childlike trust, we each grabbed our bag and took the hand of a stranger who walked us to her car to begin our new lives—a life that would endure more loss, repeated rejection, and unthinkable abuse.

Yet, decades later, I'd again face the opportunity for that childlike trust. Except this time, it would not be as a six-year-old taking a stranger's hand, but a forty-six-year-old grabbing tightly to the hand of her Deliverer. Like Mary Magdalene, God had called me by name, and I was His. He was my Healer. My Protector. My Provider.

During this next season of abandonment by people I trusted, my heavenly Father held me securely. His everlasting arms protected me as I experienced betrayal by the senior and associate pastors of my church of thirty-three years, and I lost my much-loved job at the church. I also lost my marriage of twenty-one years when my husband walked away from everything, even our three teenage children. He almost emptied our bank account, leaving me with only $1,800. I had no job, and he left me with all the bills. I had to rebuild my life.

But God. He used all of these betrayals and losses to bring me to the place of asking two questions that would forever change my life:

Who am I?

What am I doing here?

Within those two questions, I would begin a journey of healing and finding significance as I discovered both my true identity and my purpose. I learned that my identity was not in who I am, but in *whose* I am.

Once an orphan—abandoned, abused, and rejected— He called my name ... *Chosen, Daughter!* What others intended for evil, He has worked for my good. Now I'm living out my purpose of bringing Him glory through the calling God had planned for me before the foundation of the world. I serve with an international women's ministry, Love UnVeiled, which helps women become the people God created them to be. Through transformational discipleship, women are able to experience the same healing and freedom I experienced. Additionally, God has provided a career I never dreamed of—serving Christian authors as a co-owner of Redemption Press, a hybrid publishing house committed to excellence and integrity in publishing.

He has turned my ashes into beauty and adorned me with the garment of praise (Isaiah 61:3). I've learned to live single-in-Christ—securely held by my heavenly Father. Like Mary, I am resting in my ultimate significance as daughter of the King!

Securely Held

A Prayer for His Beloved

Dear heavenly Father, I praise You that You have a plan for the church, Your bride, and for every individual member You have called and chosen. Your plan is not for evil but for good. You promise a glorious future for each of Your children. I pray I will understand that my significance was sealed with Christ's blood when You called me by name. Father, please give me hope amid whatever I am facing—not hope in people, circumstances, or myself, but hope in You. As you revealed Yourself to Mary Magdalene, You hear my cries. You see my tears and tenderly call to me to look up. As I see Your face, may I find significance and security in Your embrace. In Jesus's name, amen.

Questions for Reflection

1. Describe a time in your life that looked very different from how you pictured it should.

2. Has a life-altering event left you searching for significance? Read Jeremiah 29:11. What three promises do you see revealed for you?

3. Read John 20:15–20. At what point does Mary Magdalene recognize Jesus? How do Jesus's words, "I am ascending to my Father and your Father, to my God and your God," reveal Mary's significance?

4. Have you ever found your significance through church instead of through Christ? What was the result?

5. Go to your Redeemer and Creator in prayer and meditate on Isaiah 43:1, which says, "But now thus says the Lord, he who created you, O Jacob, he who formed you, O Israel: 'Fear not, for I have redeemed you; I have called you by name, you are mine.'"

Finding Rest in God's Embrace

Chapter Nine

Why Am I So Tired?

Bear one another's burdens,
and so fulfill the law of Christ.

GALATIANS 6:2

"Cheryl, you are a pastor's wife. You're homeschooling your children and teaching ladies' Bible study. You've just had your fourth baby! You are constantly exercising hospitality by hosting missionary families and groups for lunch almost every Sunday. My admiration for you just continues to grow!"

We were standing on the steps outside the stately old church building. I was wearing a lovely floral dress my mother-in-law had bought for me, and my eight-, six-, and four-year-old children were standing at my feet wearing their Sunday best. I may not have had time for breakfast that morning, but I made sure I had my makeup applied and my hair brushed and clipped back with a lovely barrette. I wondered if the man delivering the compliment could hear my stomach growling as I shifted the handle of the baby carrier from side to side. It grew heavier by the minute with little one-month-old Joey snuggled inside. I wanted to burst into tears and tell this man

I was an impostor and that things weren't how they appeared. But, instead, I flashed my warm smile and hoped he would overlook the pain behind my eyes.

You see, I was exhausted with a capital E. After I returned to my faith in my early twenties, I dated and married my amazing pastor husband and soon after began having children, all while living a fishbowl existence. Subconsciously, instead of fighting to prove myself and earn validation from the world, I thought I could sanctify my people-pleasing tendencies and need for validation by sacrificial Christian service.

Just a few short months after that morning on the church steps, the near-perfect health I had experienced for most of my life took a nosedive. The seizures, chronic fatigue, and muscle weakness began with a vengeance. My relentless efforts to prove myself as a pastor's wife and a homeschooling mom were zapping me physically, spiritually, and emotionally, and I didn't even recognize it.

What about you? Has serving and pleasing others left you burned out and at your breaking point? When you finally have time away with your family or friends, is your mind on your to-do list the entire time? Together, let's explore some possible reasons why.

False Burden-Bearing

Part of the reason I was burned out and broken was that I was carrying burdens not meant for me to hold. Always striving to meet others' needs, I used Scripture to support my people-pleasing behavior. Galatians 6:2 urges us, "Bear one another's burdens, and so fulfill the law of Christ." In the name of *fulfilling the law of Christ*, I found myself taking on the physical or emotional demands of those around me. While this verse encourages us to serve others by being the hands and feet of Jesus, it does not require us to assume the role of Jesus and create a dependency on us instead of Christ.

Burden-bearing must be done in a way that is healthy for us, helpful to the recipient, and most importantly, glorifying to God. Carrying burdens not meant for us is unhealthy and stressful to our minds and bodies. Our families suffer as well when our mental and physical health suffers. It's important to realize that bearing one another's burdens does not mean carrying someone's burden, which would enable them to walk away from their responsibility and cause them to look to us instead of Jesus to meet their needs. When we view it from this angle, we see how it dishonors God when we enable His people instead of allowing them to learn the lessons He is trying to teach them.

Pleasing People vs. Loving People

I discovered another reason I was so exhausted; I was confusing pleasing people with loving people. This is also a form of false burden-bearing, because the burden of keeping others happy is not on us. We are always called to love others, but loving people in a biblical way will not always please them. In fact, sometimes it's quite the opposite. For years my thoughts and actions orbited around keeping people happy, never ceasing in my attempts to meet expectations—stressful, exhausting, unattainable, and sinful.

Marshall Segal, a staff writer for *Desiring God*, said, "The sin of people-pleasing, almost by definition, presumes duplicity. If we're constantly angling to do what pleases others, it is almost impossible to remain consistent or maintain integrity (especially if we're trying to please several people at once). That means one way we battle people-pleasing is to prize and protect *sincerity*."[27]

When our whole focus is on rearranging our words and actions in a way to please others—especially more than one person at a time—we inevitably become insincere. He offers that one way to win the fight against people-pleasing is to check ourselves to see if we're being truthful. An example of this is a story I remember hearing years ago (I don't recall where) about a husband who heard his wife on the phone in what sounded like a happy conversation. Upon hanging up the phone, however, she began to complain about how she would have to rearrange her entire schedule the next day to complete the last-minute task she had just agreed to on the phone. Her husband listened quietly before responding, "Why did you just tell Susie you were happy to do it and that it was no problem at all?" Friend, our integrity suffers when we lie to keep the peace or make others happy, and it leads to emotional and physical exhaustion.

When our priority is saying yes to God that sometimes means saying no to people. And when your people have always known you as the *yes girl*, saying no to them rocks their world, and they don't like it. Biblical love says yes to the ways God is calling you to serve and no to the things He is not calling you to do. We cannot allow people's negative responses to change our answers. Saying no in love pushes others to look outside their circle for help, which brings growth and the opportunity for someone else to experience the privilege of serving.

God had to teach me to lay down the burden of people-pleasing amid physical, mental, and emotional exhaustion. The solution to false burden-bearing is biblical burden-bearing, which enables us to fulfill the law of Christ by loving God and others the way our Savior intended.

Let God Work

Looking for approval from other people leads to desperate striving, while putting our focus on God's glory leads to a restful pursuit of what pleases Him. Marshall Segal says, "The people-pleaser desperately chases the wills of other people; the God-fearer focuses on discerning and pursuing the will of God."[28] When my health fell apart, I was forced to rest and learn to seek God's will before saying yes to something.

Here's an example. A woman called and asked me to consider being the chairwoman of the women's ministry team. I prayed about her request first but didn't feel God calling me to take on any new leadership responsibilities. When she called back, I ended up telling her no. She wasn't happy with my no and replied that it was her conviction that the pastor's wife should serve on the leadership team. My health was still not strong, so I knew I had to obey God and not the desires of others, even though the previous pastor's wife had *always* served on the women's board. God used my no to show the women that the pastor's wife doesn't have to be involved in everything. My refusal also allowed the other ladies the opportunity to exercise their God-given gifts.

In another example, I saw firsthand how a young family was blessed by hosting a missionary family. I was not feeling well, so this young couple volunteered to have the missionaries stay in their home instead of ours. The missionary wife was able to minister to the host wife, who was grieving over her infertility, connecting with her over her own infertility story. If I had said yes to hosting them out of a burden to please or prove, I would have denied this hurting couple this healing balm.

Securely Held

Moses Learns to Rest

> But Moses' hands grew weary, so they took a stone and put
> it under him, and he sat on it, while Aaron and Hur held
> up his hands, one on one side, and the other on the other
> side. So his hands were steady until the going down of the
> sun. **Exodus 17:12**

We see a poignant example of biblical burden-bearing in Israel's battle with the Amalekites. Moses allows Aaron and Hur to come alongside him and hold up his arms amid the fight, providing Moses the opportunity to sit down on a rock, rest, and regain his strength. As Moses receives their support, God provides the strength to lead the Israelites to victory.

Biblical burden-bearing means coming alongside someone when you observe them being crushed under the weight of their load. Notice how Aaron and Hur didn't tell Moses to go home and leave the whole weight of the battle to them. Instead, they let him sit down and rest, each bearing him up under an armpit. Aaron and Hur obeyed the call to bear one another's burdens, and Moses obeyed God's call to rest and allow others to help.

My friend Melony Brown's book *Challenges Won't Stop Me: An Interactive Survival Guide for Overcoming and Thriving*, provides readers with the necessary encouragement to persevere through the toughest of life's challenges. Melony is the perfect example of perseverance. However, in the following story, she shares how God taught her the significance of rest and accepting help from others during a health crisis.

Just a few months before turning forty, my first mini-stroke attacked my body and brain without any kind of warning. It had been thirty-eight years since my stroke at age two. I'd learned to navigate life well despite a weaker left side and difficulties with balance, coordination, and word retrieval—so much so that most people were often shocked to learn I had suffered a significant stroke as a toddler.

During my six-week recovery after my mini-stroke at age thirty-nine, family and friends lavished us with love and food, prayed for me, and encouraged me when several of the effects lingered, specifically the unrelenting fatigue. Over the next four years, three more mini-strokes caused the fatigue to worsen. I loved my job as a teacher, but a full day of teaching now meant an hourlong nap afterward. Prayer tethered me to the only one who could possibly understand my immense frustration about a lifetime of dealing with neurological struggles and the ways each neurological incident impacted my body and brain. The fatigue tested my positive attitude and perseverance. "How much longer will I have to endure this?" I cried out time and time again. God, in His infinite wisdom, chose not to answer. Instead of being angered by His silence, I drew closer to Him.

Time spent in solitude and silence opened my eyes to all the ways He provided, strengthened, and equipped me throughout my life. Even though God hates to see us hurting, I knew those struggles were teaching me invaluable truths. One of the many truths fatigue taught me is that taking time to rest was part of God's plan from the very beginning. He created the world in six days, and on the seventh day, He rested (Genesis 2:2–3). If He needed rest, and even commanded it for us (Exodus 20:11), then who was I to not follow His example? My body and brain were screaming that they needed rest, so I rested.

After my fourth mini-stroke, an angiogram of my brain revealed a rare, progressive cerebrovascular disease, called *moyamoya*, had formed in my brain while I was in my mother's womb. The neurosurgeon explained that a tangle of blood vessels in my brain caused my stroke at age two, the decades of debilitating migraines, and the four mini-strokes. Finally learning the name for my lifetime of neurological struggles silenced the voice in my head that said, *You're making up these symptoms. You just want attention.* To slow the progression of my rare disease, my neurosurgeon moved a thriving blood vessel in my brain to the area that hadn't received blood flow all my life.

Following brain surgery in March of 2016, I experienced a surge of energy due to the increased blood flow in my brain. God's healing was miraculous! I felt fantastic when I returned after surgery to finish the school year. Because I knew I would need sustained energy to teach in the fall, I deliberately rested during the summer, and I felt great when school began in August. Unfortunately, the constant demand on my brain invited the fatigue to return. My body was tired at the end of a school day, but my brain was far more than tired. I was exhausted. Each day, two- to three-hour naps became a necessity. My frustration turned to anger over losing two to three hours every evening with my family.

By early October, I was forced to admit my energy, focus, and delivery of lessons were great in the mornings but would tank just after lunch each day. It was clear that my neurological struggles were impacting my ability to teach. I was not okay with that, so I shared my concerns and frustrations with my husband. Even though I didn't have enough sick days to cover a month-long leave of absence, he agreed it was necessary. We believed God would somehow provide. I met with my principal, and she approved a month of personal leave for me to rest.

The week leading up to my leave of absence, I chatted with several of the other teachers, describing how hopeful I felt about having a dedicated time of rest for my body and brain. Each conversation ended with words of encouragement and promises of prayer. I met with the school's finance director as my last stop before heading home for a month. In a truthful but kind way, she pointed out the number of sick days I had banked versus the number of days I would be out during my leave of absence. I pushed her words to the back of my mind.

Ten hours or more of sleep each night plus long naps each day affirmed what I believed my body and brain were telling me: they needed rest. My waking hours were brightened by silly text messages, voicemails ending with prayer, and cards filled with encouraging words from coworkers, friends, and family. Words from Shelly Miller's book *Rhythms of Rest,* nourished my mind: "A forced Sabbath is a ruthless grace, pulling us out of danger in order to move forward at a slower pace."[29] (I do believe that rest pulled me out of danger, preventing other neurological events.)

When I met with the school financial adviser upon my return, she rejoiced with me about how beneficial that month of rest proved to be. She handed me an envelope and said, "Open it at home this evening with your husband." Neither Jeff nor I were prepared for the words on the card. It read, *For each day of your leave of absence, one teacher voluntarily donated one of their sick days so you wouldn't be without income while you rested. Your school family loves you.*

We were so grateful. God provided in the most beautiful way. My school family exemplified Galatians 6:10 (NIV): "Therefore, as we have opportunity, let us do good to all people, especially to those who belong to the family of believers." May we follow their beautiful example.

Why Am I So Tired?

Finding Rest in the Security of God's Embrace

The late evangelist Billy Graham had remarkable insight into burden-bearing: "Everyone is designed to be able to assume his own individual level of responsibilities and pressures. But when his load goes beyond the breaking point, another is to come along and help—and sometimes that help can be given through the sharing of our time and material possessions."[30]

We are called by Christ to come alongside those who are at their breaking point, sharing our time or possessions. We are also called to allow others to help us when we are at our breaking point. Melony's coworkers who shared their sick days with her, so she wouldn't be without income while she rested, is a lovely example of what Graham is saying.

Joni Eareckson Tada, in her memoir titled *The God I Love: A Lifetime of Walking with Jesus,* shares her experience with quadriplegia and her struggle to understand why God allows suffering. Her friend offered the following perspective about the ways of God: "He permits things he hates—really hates—to accomplish something he loves."[31] Through our individual health crises, Melony and I have each learned this characteristic of God. God permitted the health challenges to accomplish His will in our lives. The forced rest caused us to press into our heavenly Father and find security and shelter in His embrace.

Friend, He wants the same for you! What is He permitting in your life in order to accomplish what He loves? Are you carrying burdens that are not yours to carry? I encourage you to kneel in prayer, hold out your arms, then lay the load at the foot of the cross.

Do you hear the Savior calling you? "Come to me, all who labor and are heavy laden, and I will give you rest. Take my yoke upon you, and learn from me, for I am gentle and lowly in heart, and you will find rest for your souls. For my yoke is easy, and my burden is light" (Matthew 11:28–30).

A Prayer for His Beloved

Dear heavenly Father, I praise You for inviting us to come to You when we are weary and burdened, and You promise to give us rest. I pray I will release burdens that are not mine to carry. I pray You will show me any areas where I am operating out of fear rather than faith. Like You gently showed Melony You were calling her to rest, please help me put my trust in You to provide for all my needs if it is time for me to step back for a season of rest. May I allow ones to come alongside me, and in humility accept their help as from Your hand. Father, comfort and strengthen me with the truth that our burdens are lifted at Calvary! Your redeeming love removed my load and placed it on Your Son. Give me a truly grateful heart. In love, may I respond by coming alongside others as Your hands and feet! In Jesus's name, amen.

Questions for Reflection

1. Describe a time you felt overwhelmed and exhausted. Consider the burdens you are bearing, and write down two that might not be yours to carry.
2. Read Galatians 6:2. What does it mean to bear one another's burdens?
3. Read Matthew 11:28–30. What is this passage saying and how does it encourage you?
4. What do you think about Joni Eareckson Tada's quote "God permits what He hates to accomplish what He loves"?
5. What is a practical step you can take today to either come alongside someone who needs support or allow someone to come alongside you?

Chapter Ten

Why Can't I Ask for Help?

When Moses's father-in-law saw all that he was doing for the people, he said, "What is this that you are doing for the people? Why do you sit alone, and all the people stand around you from morning till evening?"

EXODUS 18:14

When I heard the doorbell ring at 11:30 a.m., my first thought was to duck down, stay quiet, and not go near the windows, threatening my kids within an inch of their lives if they did not do the same. I was still in my nightgown, no makeup and unwashed hair, and I hadn't even brushed my teeth that morning. I was still driven by the opinions of others, and I wanted to escape the situation and prevent this unexpected visitor from seeing me when I wasn't looking my best. I was barely functioning on this particular day not long after those undiagnosed bizarre physical symptoms had entered my life.

Before I could warn the kids to take part in my tactics, however, my plan was foiled when my precious offspring sprang for the front door with delight, having seen their dear Mrs. Vitkus's car in the driveway. Pat, a recent widow, was like a second grandmother to our children and a second mother to me. This dear friend and mentor had come bearing gifts of homemade broccoli cheese soup and fresh, warm loaves of carb comfort. I soon learned she had been driving between appointments in town when the Lord placed my children and me on her heart. So she followed the Lord's promptings, pulled into The Bread Basket, my favorite restaurant in Hammond, Indiana, and picked up some lunch for us.

Her warm smile quickly faded as she sensed the weakness in my body and saw the exhaustion behind my eyes. Compassion without judgment radiated from her, noticing that my kids and I were still clad in our pajamas at almost noon. She slowly made her way inside with her delivery, carefully stepping over Abigail's naked Barbie dolls, who *always* seemed to be undressed when company came to call. Then as Pat cautiously made her way around baby Joey sleeping in his swing, her eyes searched our tiny kitchen in vain for an empty spot to set down our food. Dirty dishes were piled in the sink and across our minimal counter space, and Hannah and Daniel's school books haphazardly covered the kitchen table. She explained she couldn't stay and help me that day because of commitments with her grandchildren, but she hoped we would enjoy her lunch delivery. After glancing again at my grubby kitchen, she slowly exhaled and sighed. Her unspoken words communicated empathy and her regret that she couldn't stay and clean. Then amid the kids' cries for her to stay, she planted a kiss on top of each messy bedhead and promised to return soon. Before exiting, she enfolded me in her arms and whispered, "Oh, Cheryl, you need a mother."

Why Can't I Ask for Help?

As the kids stood at the window waving goodbye, the sweet aroma of freshly baked bread wafted through our small Cape Cod home. The smell of savory sustenance did bring comfort in the chaos around me, like a Holy Spirit hug. But as Joey began stirring in his swing, I listened to the squeaking and creaking battery-operated babysitter—which had survived his three older siblings—gliding back and forth to the tune of "Mary Had a Little Lamb." I thought of the words to that beloved children's song:

> Mary had a little lamb whose fleece was white as snow.
> And everywhere that Mary went,
> the lamb was sure to go.
> It followed her to school one day,
> which was against the rules.
> It made the children laugh and play,
> to see a lamb at school.[32]

I thought of how our homeschooled kids would talk about "real school" and what fun it would be to have a pet follow them. I explained to them that what we were doing was a real school, but days like today made me question if that were true. I initially believed I could keep the platters spinning—ministry, schooling, hospitality, and a new baby. But the plates were rudely landing all around me, like the dirty dishes piled in my sink. I could not keep up the pace of working from morning till evening, especially with my health issues, but I didn't know how to admit that fact to myself or anyone else. Nor did I know how to ask for help.

In Exodus 18:14–27, we see that Moses didn't know how to ask for help or even realize he needed it. We read that he was acting as the sole judge of the Israelites, meeting with the people daily, from morning till evening. The man clearly did not know the meaning of the word delegate!

Like Moses, my friend Phylis Mantelli didn't know how to ask for help either. Her mother struggled with alcoholism and narcissistic tendencies, and she burdened Phylis, from a very young age, with responsibilities that were not hers to carry. You can read about Phylis's harrowing journey to break generational patterns and provide hope and healing for the next generation in her memoir, *Unmothered: Life With a Mom Who Couldn't Love Me.*

Below, Phylis shares a portion of her story about learning to relinquish control and let others help:

> As I sat by the phone waiting for results from the hospital for my dad, it occurred to me how this situation had all played out. My brother happened to stop by my father's house to check up on him. My dad embarrassingly told him he didn't feel good "down there." After hearing my dad describe his very painful symptoms, my brother rushed him to the hospital. Once there, it was discovered that Dad had a very enlarged prostate. As was protocol with the COVID-19 pandemic at the time, only one person was allowed to stay with the patient. Since my brother had brought him in, he was the one.
>
> Why was this such an issue with me? I quickly discovered that I still had some control issues from growing up in this dysfunctional family. I had been the sole child who always ran to help when my parents

needed me. I cooked, cleaned, paid their bills, and fixed any problems. It was an agreement made in silence that I was the responsible child. However, I was exhausted! Not only had I been caring for my parents most of my life, but I had also been caring for my family, helping at church, volunteering for the homeless, writing a book, and more. The list went on and on. I was getting older and more burned out each day. I just didn't know how to relinquish control. From a young age, I had been taught to "toughen up" and handle everything that came my way.

This was probably much like Moses felt, I'm sure, when all the people came to him for help. We get a glimpse to his feelings in his answer to his father-in-law when asked what he was doing sitting alone, from morning till evening, with all the people standing around him. "And Moses said to his father-in-law, 'Because the people come to me to inquire of God; when they have a dispute, they come to me and I decide between one person and another; I make them know the statutes of God and his laws'" **(Exodus 18:15–16).**

Friend, just because our intentions are good doesn't mean we must handle everything all ourselves. Moses also had to learn this lesson, and his father-in-law gave him sound advice: "Moses's father-in-law said to him, 'What you are doing is not good. You and the people with you will certainly wear yourselves out, for the thing is too heavy for you. You are not able to do it alone'" **(Exodus 18:17–18).**

Like Moses, I needed to know that I could not do it alone. And as scary as that day with my father was, it was a blessing in disguise. God showed me that my father was not my sole responsibility. Like Moses, I needed to let others come alongside and help … such as my brother. He has taken over the daily tasks and care of my father since then. For the first time in my life, I was able to simply visit my father and be a daughter who could spend quality time with him instead of worrying about all the details. It freed me up to take care of others in my immediate family too. Sometimes good things must be shared to let others shine.

I now ask God to allow me to see where I must release control and the thought of doing it all myself. I ask Him to let me see where someone may be in the wings of wanting to help, and my desire for control could be keeping them from coming forward. I'm grateful that He opens my eyes to rest in His comfort and trust in Him alone.

Acceptable Options vs. Biblical Mandates

As Phylis learned to relinquish control and allow her brother and others to help, Moses likewise heeded the exhortation of his father-in-law, Jethro. He released his control by training and entrusting godly men to bear the burden alongside him.

Jon Bloom, a staff writer at DesiringGod.org, says,

God speaks with clarity and preciseness everything that is required to redeem his people and make them holy throughout the generations. He's clear on every commandment to be obeyed and every promise to be trusted. But regarding secondary or administrative things, he leaves much to our figuring out. He loves to answer our prayers for guidance in these areas, but he almost always answers indirectly. He does not want us to make an idol out of what is only meant to be helpful.[33]

I believe Bloom is saying that God doesn't want us to place our hope in systems. In other words, there are different ways of accomplishing our God-given assignments if no sin is involved. We shouldn't mandate that everyone use the same method we do if it's not prescribed in God's Word.

Likewise, Bloom's words remind me of a lesson I had to learn about homeschooling all those years ago when I had made an idol out of a method. You see, homeschooling is a wonderfully viable option for educating our children. I have friends and loved ones who accomplished homeschooling (or are currently accomplishing it) with excellence. They have happy, though imperfect, homes where their kids are thriving. But sadly, the atmosphere in our home was stressful during those early years of homeschooling while my health was poor. The kids were ahead of the curve academically in most subjects in their primary years, but they were struggling in other areas. Daniel especially needed more stimulation for his logical male mind, and he was frustrated surrounded by his mother and sisters all day. And my exhaustion and sickness put too much pressure on dear Hannah, our first-born daughter.

Thankfully we also have some great memories of our early home-learning journey—daily escapes to faraway lands during story time, the thrill of teaching our older three to read, the flexibility of taking family vacations during the "off season" for pastors.

Homeschooling is one method among several, yet not a sacred system. When my kids were young, my motive for homeschooling was believing that it was my duty before God and what was expected of me by others. Pure duty, or going through the motions but lacking a loving spirit, is ugly. Especially after becoming sick, I was overwhelmed by the task I thought God was commanding me to do. I did not have family support or a network of home educators in the area. Yet I believed what some taught regarding Deuteronomy 6:6–8: "You shall teach them diligently to your children, and shall talk of them when you sit in your house, and when you walk by the way, and when you lie down, and when you rise." Some people interpret the verses to mean children should spend most of their day with their parents, thus they mandate homeschooling. The passage indeed instructs us to school our children in God's commands diligently and naturally throughout our daily activities. However, God had to show me that my husband and I could faithfully teach our children His commands without taking on the entirety of their education. I did not have to do it all alone.

God also had to show me that one of my motives for homeschooling was to receive a desired outcome. It was almost like a silent bargain I had with God. *I will sacrifice my needs and wants and homeschool my kids so You will guarantee they grow into God-fearing, ministry-minded adolescents and then adults. And because of all I'm giving up for my family, You will keep me healthy and ensure parenting and educating my children goes smoothly.* I thought I had a bulletproof method, but that thinking reminds me of an old song: "(I Never Promised You a) Rose Garden."

Friend, God never promised us a rose garden with raising our children or any other part of life. Instead, He guaranteed struggle. In John 16:33, Jesus tells his disciples, "I have said these things to you, that in me you may have peace. In the world you will have tribulation. But take heart; I have overcome the world." Trying to earn God's favor and blessing and believing we can avoid struggles is stinkin' thinking. As Baptist preacher and expositor Alexander MacLaren (1826–1910) said, "Peace comes not from the absence of troubles, but from the presence of God."[34]

When we feel overwhelmed and lack peace in our lives, we need to examine our motives before God and ask Him if there is anything we need to release control over.

Relinquishing Control

I'm incredibly grateful for my soup-bearing spiritual mother, Pat, who later challenged me the way Jethro challenged Moses. She showed me I was wearing myself out and could not do it all alone. She encouraged me to release control and enlist help. In love, she confronted me with the fact that our current schooling situation was not what was best for our kids. Pat even appealed to the elders of our church on our behalf, and they agreed to provide us with an education stipend. This enabled us to enroll our older two in a nearby Christian school. After some adjustments, our children began to thrive in their new environment. I was able to get some needed rest and spend quality time with the younger two.

Friend, there are varying reasons why we struggle to ask for help or fail to delegate, running ourselves ragged. Here are a few reasons to consider:

- Fear: If you grew up in a home where you experienced emotional neglect, you likely have trust issues. You fear trusting others to help you because you are accustomed to figuring things out independently. And if you trust and delegate something to someone, they might fail or disappoint you.

- Insecurity: If we are insecure in our identity as God's daughter, we crave the appearance of having it all together. Our insecurity drives us to prove to others that we can do it all alone. And if we delegate, it might make us look as weak or inadequate as we feel.

- Control: When we fail to rest in God's sovereignty, we become control freaks. We believe that if we arrange all the chess pieces ourselves, we can design the outcome. And if we delegate, something might be done wrong, and our carefully laid plans will fail.

These reasons are not healthy and leave us in bondage. God designed us to function in community, not alone. Let's look at some practical strategies to help us overcome these barriers so we can experience rest by asking for help:

1. Realize that, yes, people will fail us and disappoint us. But God has promised never to leave us or forsake us. We can receive other people's imperfect help without putting our

hope in them. Rather, we place our hope in God's perfect presence, while allowing others to come alongside us.

2. Remember, we are secure in God's love and acceptance. We have nothing left to prove to Him, ourselves, or others. Admitting our weaknesses enables us to ask for help, and it breaks the power of people's opinions.

3. Rest in the fact that we are not called to control the outcomes in life. Rather, we are called to obey and follow the principles in God's Word and leave the outcome to Him. We can lay our heads on the firm promise that He is working all things for our good and His glory. We should likewise heed the advice of Stonewall Jackson, who said, "Never take counsel of your fears."[35] Instead, let's release our fears and allow others to help carry the load.

A Prayer for His Beloved

Dear heavenly Father, I praise You for Your tender love and care for each of Your children. You did not leave us as orphans but instead gave us Your Holy Spirit to dwell with us. Father, please help me to know that You do not want me isolated and striving to do everything myself. You created us to live our lives in a community of believers, and You want us to allow others to come alongside us and help carry the load. Please help me trust You with the outcome as I release my fear, insecurity, and control. In Jesus's name, amen.

Questions for Reflection

1. Describe a time in your life when you experienced burnout or felt overwhelmed.
2. Do you wrestle with asking for help? Why or why not?
3. Is there something God is asking you to delegate or release control over?
4. Write out a prayer to God based on Stonewall Jackson's quote, "Never take counsel of your fears."
5. Look up Hebrews 10:24–25. Write out a practical way you can live out these verses this week.

Chapter Eleven

Why Am I So Anxious?

Show hospitality to one another
without grumbling.

1 PETER 4:9

I wrapped the curly cord around my index finger and wedged the phone between my chin and right shoulder. The cheerfulness in my voice dissipated as my in-laws explained they would not be coming the next day as planned. I suddenly felt the stress of the day throughout my entire body. I slowly dropped onto the kitchen chair, my shoulders slouching forward. *They're not coming,* I mouthed to my husband as he entered the room, and I handed him the receiver.

I stood up and carefully stepped over the flexible spiral cord, which stretched across our tiny kitchen to our landline attached to the wall in the hallway. I crossed over into the living room and clumsily melted into our secondhand velour sofa. What started as a few tears gliding down my cheeks rapidly progressed into an ugly cry. Judging from the unsightly mixture of mascara and mucus, one would have thought I had just heard the news of death or disaster. My hubby, quite bewildered by my uncharacteristic overreaction, quickly ended the phone call with his parents. He then picked up a box of tissues from one of the end tables and gingerly handed me one. He sought to understand my emotional outburst over his parents canceling their plans to come to stay with us for the weekend to celebrate his birthday.

Was I crying because I felt sorry for him or because I knew how disappointed the kids would be? Sadly, while both those things played a role, the main reason for my tears was self-pity. All that hard work preparing for my husband's birthday celebration, and it would just be our little family to taste and see the fruits of my labors. I know, somebody get the violin!

Scripture tells us to practice hospitality without complaining, but preparing for guests can sometimes bring about exhaustion and an anxious mood in us. We have looked at the life of Moses and seen that bearing burdens that are not ours to carry and trying to do it all ourselves can make us too anxious to rest. Perhaps we're trying to do too much or our motives for serving are misplaced. When we make hospitality and the other tasks of our day about ourselves instead of others, it becomes more about impressing and earning approval than serving and leads to burnout and anxiety.

A source of my exhaustion that day before my husband's fortieth birthday was a *circle cake* with browned butter icing. Let me explain, round cakes became our family joke after having dinner at the home of some of our parishioners. The hostess, Marion, had served up a delicious three-course meal that would have put a five-star restaurant to shame. But what really captivated our children was the lovely homemade two-layer chocolate cake with buttercream frosting she set before us for dessert. Our little three-year-old Abigail's mouth dropped open with wonder, and her eyes were wide as saucers as she finally exclaimed, "Mrs. Neve, how did you get it into a circle? My mom's cakes are always square!"

Yes, I had always pressed the easy button and made the kids' birthday cakes in a rectangular pan. But for Alan's special birthday, since his parents were coming to celebrate with us, I was determined to make a two-layer round cake from scratch with homemade icing. The browned butter icing involved browning the butter in a saucepan before adding the other ingredients, and then placing the pan in a bowl of ice water. If you try and skip this thickening step, you're left with a runny mess. Nevertheless, before it was all said and done, I was ready to get the super glue (or duct tape!) to make the top layer stop sliding off the bottom. Of course, finishing up the baking that evening was just the "icing on the cake" as the rest of the day consisted of schoolwork, cleaning, changing beds, and preparing the main course and sides, all while yelling at the kids to not touch anything. Although the cake was still leaning, I had just gotten the top layer to stay in place when I took that phone call.

The main problem that day wasn't a homemade cake, however. It was that I had lost sight of what was important. While I had been distracted by all the work, I had neglected the one necessity—time in the Word with Jesus. And that reminds me of a woman named Martha.

Martha, Martha

> *But Martha was distracted with much serving. And she went up to him and said, "Lord, do you not care that my sister has left me to serve alone? Tell her then to help me."*
> **Luke 10:40**

Anxious and frustrated in her service to provide a meal and dining experience for Jesus and her other guests, Martha is running herself ragged while her sister Mary sits at the feet of Jesus, listening to him teach. Finally, in exasperation, she appeals to Jesus to make her sister help her, saying, "Lord, do you not care that my sister has left me to serve alone? Tell her then to help me" (Luke 10:40). I doubt she was expecting the answer Jesus gave her.

Instead of shooing Mary away to the kitchen to help, Jesus says, "Martha, Martha, you are anxious and troubled about many things, but one thing is necessary. Mary has chosen the good portion, which will not be taken away from her" (Luke 10:41–42). Jesus doesn't strongly rebuke Mary, as Martha was asking Him to do. Instead, He gently corrects Martha herself. He tells her she is distracted by lesser things while Mary has kept her heart and mind on the main thing.

Bloom, the staff writer for DesiringGod.org, explains that this gathering in the home of these two sisters could have possibly involved a hundred people or more. The seventy-two had just rejoined Jesus, and news about Him was widespread. Jesus's presence would likely have attracted the sisters' community as well. So, before we judge Martha, we must consider the number of guests packed into their home, with the guest of honor being Jesus Himself. I don't know about you, but it takes much less than that to distract me! In fact, Bloom says Mary is the peculiar one, not Martha: "It seems to me that Martha isn't the strange person in this story. Mary is. What's remarkable is that Mary *wasn't* distracted. She ignored the insistent to-do lists so she could listen to Jesus."[36]

Friend, how often do we do the opposite of Mary?

While ignoring Jesus and neglecting our reading and prayer time, we listen to our to-do list instead, allowing it to distract and consume us. When we feel anxious and distracted while serving in our home, church, or community, we need to examine our motives. Are we serving to either gain approval, impress others, or please people? Bloom also observes, "To just about everyone else present, Martha's serving probably appeared to flow from a gracious servant's heart. But Jesus discerned differently. He saw that Martha was serving out of anxiety, not grace."[37] I appreciate Bloom's point and think we should ask ourselves the same question: Are we serving out of grace or anxiety? An emotional outburst when the unexpected intersects with our plan is a good indicator that our heart is tipping toward anxious rather than peaceful serving.

My friend Missy Eversole has written an excellent book, *Transformed, Not Conformed: Embracing a Life-Changing Approach to Spiritual Habits*, on discovering a peaceful heart through developing spiritual habits. Below Missy shares how an embarrassing meltdown led her to seek the one thing needed—a peaceful heart—eventually helping her even to birth a book on the subject.

> Have you ever had a meltdown in the parking lot of your children's school?
>
> Our sweet little angels are oblivious to the fact that we are impatiently waiting for them to come out those school doors so we can drive them to the next stop on their sports and activities list. They only become aware of our impatience when they see their mom having a meltdown in the parking lot.
>
> I'm that mom who had a meltdown, and it was in front of students, teachers, and parents. It wasn't my finest

moment of parenting. Yes, my boys were late getting out of school, but for a good reason—they stayed after to help a teacher. But I was so focused on getting to our next destination on time, I erupted with anger because we would be late for soccer practice again.

At that time in my life, I was physically tired, emotionally drained, and spiritually depleted. As a people-pleaser, setting boundaries wasn't in my vocabulary, so when someone asked me to volunteer to do something, I did it. I strived to be viewed as *Pinterest-perfect* and a woman who could juggle everything effortlessly on her jammed-packed calendar.

By letting my desire to please others rule, my spiritual life was in a drought and lukewarm. The fire I once had for Christ was almost extinguished. I was going through the motions with my relationship with Him. I showed up for church, filled in the blanks for the women's Bible study book, and that was it. I did the bare minimum.

My family no longer had a happy wife and mom but a stressed-out, stretched-thin wife and mom. I was a Pinterest failure.

After my epic meltdown in the parking lot, I knew I needed a significant life change. Being most concerned with how other people viewed me had become my idol.

The following day, I found myself back in that same parking lot, phone in hand, scrolling through social media and contemplating how to build my relationship with Jesus again. At that moment, the Holy Spirit reminded me of the Bible I kept in my purse. It looked well-worn and used, almost as if I read it daily. The truth is it looked that way because I moved it from purse to purse, dropping everything from keys to my wallet on it. The inside pages were crisp and clean because I had never opened it and read the precious words it contained.

I turned to the easiest verse I could remember, John 3:16: "For God so loved the world, that he gave his only Son, that whoever believes in him should not perish but have eternal life."

God gave His Son for me to have eternal life! I knew right then that my people-pleasing days were over, and I needed to live a life for Christ. It was the beginning of my transformation of saying no to others and yes to Jesus.

From that day on, I started reading my Bible in the parking lot instead of scrolling mindlessly through social media. From there, I began meditating on the Word and setting aside time for prayer, silence, and solitude.

The meltdown in the middle school parking was, ironically, one of my biggest blessings. My fire reignited for Jesus, and my family had a happy wife and mom again.

My sons are young adults now, and memories of this meltdown day get discussed every now and then. Thankfully, they can laugh about it, but what they remember the most is not my screaming at them but how Jesus took their stressed-out mom and radically transformed her.

Thank you, Jesus!

Keep It Simple, Sweetie

At a ladies' retreat years ago, I attended one of the workshops on hospitality. The leader used the acronym KISS—Keep It Simple, Sweetie. It was a good lesson on swallowing our pride and keeping things simple while exercising hospitality. This is especially important when we have little ones at home or other pressing demands that limit our time.

Close your eyes and think about a time when you were a guest in someone's home. Could you feel tension when you walked in the door, with the host anxiously rushing about? If so, how did that make you feel? Or did you have a sense of peace when you entered her home? Did she make you feel relaxed and that she was happy you were there?

If you haven't been invited into anyone's home in a while, pray about whom you can invite into yours. Much of the time, the reason we fail to love our neighbors and church family by exercising hospitality is that we don't feel we have the time and energy to do so. But we must ask ourselves, is this because we are trying to make things too complicated? Or are we striving for perfection instead of being present with those Christ has called us to serve? Also, let's remember my friend Missy's story and never forfeit our time with our Savior to try to be Pinterest-perfect for others.

Friend, after my own meltdown that evening before my husband's birthday, Jesus changed my perspective as well. Some time in His Word and a good night's sleep worked wonders, waking me up to the obvious—the day was about my hubby, not about me and my need for validation. No one cared about a circle cake except me (and maybe little Abigail!). Instead, I needed to simplify things. It wasn't a season for me to learn the art of baking or cake decorating. If that were a passion (which it still *isn't!*), there would be time for that in the future when the kids were older. I needed to let go of perfection and involve my kids more in our serving (and perhaps let them help bake a cake from a mix and decorate it with canned frosting!).

Bloom reminds us of another important lesson: when we serve others, we must remember that, ultimately, we are serving Christ. He says, "Jesus's gentle rebuke of Martha was an act of love—to her and to us. We are all Marthas at times. And through this correction, Jesus is asking us: whom are *we* serving in our serving? No one's motives are ever completely pure. But when we feel compelled to serve out of a self-conscious anxiety over what others think, it's likely we are serving our own glory and not Jesus's glory."[38] I believe Bloom raises some excellent questions to ask ourselves: Whom are we serving? Is it more about ourselves or the other person? And most importantly, are we serving for God's glory or our own?

Ultimately, it was just the kids, me, and Alan for his fortieth birthday celebration. The kids had fun celebrating and serving their daddy. The birthday boy enjoyed the quiet day being loved on by his family. And my anxious, distracted heart found rest as I learned a valuable lesson: we serve others for God's glory and not our own.

Securely Held

A Prayer for His Beloved

Dear heavenly Father, please help me to take to heart these words from the old hymn "One Thing's Needful; Lord, This Treasure:"

> One thing's needful; Lord, this treasure teach me highly to regard.
>
> All else, though it first gives pleasure, is a yoke that presses hard.
>
> Beneath it, the heart is still fretting and striving, no true, lasting happiness ever deriving.
>
> This one thing is needful; all others are vain—I count all but loss that Christ I may obtain.[39]

Father, may I indeed stop striving over things that don't matter and set my eyes on You and Your glory. Please help me to realize that my most important accomplishment today is the same as Mary's—to sit at Your feet, pour out my heart, and soak in Your love. In Jesus's name, amen.

Questions for Reflection

1. Describe a time you felt stretched thin from serving others. Why do you think you were so exhausted?
2. Read Luke 10:41–42. Do you relate more to Mary or Martha? Why?
3. Read 1 Peter 4:9. Are you exercising hospitality? Are you doing so without complaining? Why or why not?
4. Read Psalm 119:148. Do you anticipate with joy times to meditate on God's Word? Why or why not?
5. Spend some time meditating on the words to the hymn "One Thing's Needful" in the prayer above.

Chapter Twelve

Where Do I Find Healing and Rest?

But they who wait for the Lord shall renew their strength; they shall mount up with wings like eagles; they shall run and not be weary; they shall walk and not faint.

ISAIAH 40:31

"There is nothing physically or organically wrong with you. All your tests are within the normal range. Also, it would be best to consider how frightening these episodes are to your children and get help. We can arrange for you to see one of our psychiatrists on staff."

Those were the words spoken to me by a neurologist when I was thirty-three years old when we were serving the church in northwest Indiana. She did not say them with grace or compassion but, instead, with rebuke and judgment. Her tone and body language made me feel like a naughty two-year-old being scolded for acting out for attention or like an unfit mother who had no regard for traumatizing her children. And the disdain in her inflection was humiliating as she explained to me why I shouldn't *want* to have *a terrible disease*. But, of course, I didn't want to have a terrible illness—I just wanted answers and hope!

My health had fallen apart several months after our fourth child's birth. I had gone to this diagnostic hospital seeking help for these bizarre symptoms that had invaded my life. Instead, I left filled with shame and hopelessness. I wanted to go home, crawl into bed, and pull the covers over my head. That wasn't an option, however, because my four young children eagerly awaited me there, and they desperately wanted their mother back. They wanted the mother who didn't spend the afternoons in bed, the mother who would read to them and act out their favorite stories, the mother who could drive them to the park and to play dates with friends, the mother who wasn't cranky and impatient all the time.

But their mommy didn't return home with renewed energy and hope that day. Instead, I came back downcast and even more exhausted than ever. Once again wrapped in shame, I believed I was a failure as a wife, mother, and ministry leader. I wanted to prove—even to myself—that I wasn't just lazy or crazy. Yet what we didn't know at the time was that day at the hospital was only the beginning of a thirteen-year struggle of searching for help and answers.

My need to prove myself kept me seeking validation for my symptoms and drove me to find a new neurologist. And after more months and a myriad of diagnostic testing, I saw the confirmation I needed. This was when the new neurologist diagnosed me with myasthenia gravis (MG). He used a test the previous doctors hadn't, which showed strong proof of the neuromuscular disease. This was around six months after the first neurologist told me she had ruled out the possibility of anything organically wrong with me and around a year after the first symptoms began. Yet, as I explained previously, God wanted me to deal with the emotional and spiritual aspects of my struggles, not just the physical ones. Therefore, I would later discover that our fight wouldn't end with that diagnosis, as I had desperately hoped.

Three years after beginning treatment for MG in Indiana and experiencing some reprieve and improvement, we moved to the Atlanta area of Georgia to serve our new church. I had been feeling so much better that upon arriving at our new home and calling, I pushed MG to the back burner. I decided the *sick Cheryl* had stayed in Indiana. Initially, I didn't even seek a new neurologist. Instead, the *healthy Cheryl* jumped into my new pastor's wife role with both feet. I again felt a strong need to prove myself worthy of the calling and thought I needed to gain the love and acceptance of the new congregation. The previous pastor and his wife were so beloved that I secretly struggled with how I would ever measure up. Right away, I began teaching ladies' Bible studies, leading women's ministry, hosting the singles group, teaching children's Sunday school, etc. Then several months into our call, my health again took a nosedive, and a quest to find a new doctor in the area who believed in my symptoms and understood how to treat me began again.

Yet after finding a new neurologist, things went from bad to worse. It suddenly became apparent that my struggle for answers wasn't over. When this new doctor learned I'd been on prednisone for a few years without tapering, she sent me for a bone density scan. The test revealed osteopenia, so she felt it best to wean me off the steroid. Unfortunately, after stopping the medicine, the muscle weakness and fatigue magnified. I began having what appeared to be seizures again, and the new neurologist questioned the MG diagnosis because it is rarely associated with seizures. I accepted her assessment that I didn't have MG, but I refused to believe the seizures were purely psychological.

I was determined to find the proper diagnostician to take me seriously and discover an accurate diagnosis and treatment plan. It was an exhausting season of getting our four children adjusted to their new home, church, and Christian school. Also, I was not allowed to drive due to the almost daily convulsions. My dear husband was under tremendous stress getting established as senior pastor, making pastoral appointments, and being the full-time driver for our busy household. At the same time, he was making time to cart me to numerous doctors all over Atlanta and even to the Mayo Clinic in Florida.

After more disappointing and humiliating appointments, however, a couple of new doctors reiterated that I needed a good psychiatrist. I didn't know what to do or where to turn for help. Then one day, when I gained access to some of my medical records, I read the assessment written by the first neurologist I'd seen in the area. I realized her notes regarding my need for a psychiatric evaluation preceded me to every appointment. Also, instead of crediting the diagnosis of MG from the neurologist in Indiana, she had reviewed the report from the hospital in Illinois, which stated my issues were purely psychiatric and not organic. This was a light bulb moment: a prominent doctor in my state made an assessment, and subsequent doctors weren't likely to challenge it. When new doctors opened the door to the evaluation room to greet me for the first time, they'd already formed strong opinions about me. They had drawn judgments from reading the previous doctor's report before they had even examined me themselves.

Soon after these devastating appointments, I began to entertain the thought that the doctors were right and that I was just crazy. I felt myself sliding into the darkness of a pit of despair. I often rolled myself into a fetal position, crying to God, "If you aren't going to heal me, why won't you send me to a doctor who will believe me and help me?" Yet it seemed my heavenly Father was silent.

So I decided that if my issues were solely in my mind, I would train my mind to ignore my physical symptoms. As I vainly tried to pray away and will away my health problems, I grew weaker. The convulsions continued with a vengeance, especially at church. Once again, I was left with the shame, humiliation, and hopelessness that I'd never lead an everyday life again.

The following year was spent exhausting our resources on expensive special diets, naturopaths, chiropractors, costly supplements, detoxes, and essential oils. I even went through the expensive procedure of removing and replacing all my amalgam dental fillings when a naturopath told me I had heavy metal toxicity. But my health continued to spiral. My thirteen-year journey reminds me of a woman in Scripture who spent all her money looking to physicians for help with a humiliating health struggle, yet she only grew worse.

A Bleeding Woman Desperate for Healing

In Luke 8, we learn Jesus walked through the cities and villages, teaching about the kingdom of God. As He made His way through the crowds with His disciples, the people pressed in around Him on the

179

packed streets. In verses 43–48, we see a woman in the group who is desperate for healing. This nameless woman had been hemorrhaging for twelve years and had spent all her savings on doctors yet found no relief. I believe she must have dealt with much shame over her affliction.

According to Sue Poorman Richards and Larry Richards in their book *Every Woman in the Bible,* "Her condition made her ritually unclean, so that she could not be touched by her husband or share in the annual worship celebrations so important in Judaism. She could not go into the temple court, light the Sabbath evening candles, or participate in the Passover meal. She would have hovered, as a ghost in her home, there and yet not there."[40]

Can you imagine the humiliation of being considered unclean and untouchable even in your own home? This Jewish woman must have felt much loneliness and unworthiness being banned from participating in the customs of her people. I believe it was shame that caused her to come up behind Jesus rather than face Him and ask for help. Instead, she humbly trailed behind, concealing her presence. Finally, she saw an opportunity to outstretch her arm and lightly grasp the fringe of His garment.

Instantaneously, she experienced a miracle. The hemorrhaging she had suffered for twelve long years immediately stopped. The blood dried up, and she knew she was healed. The *untouchable woman* was suddenly cured by touching Christ's garment. Knowing that medicinal power had flowed out from him, Jesus asked, "Who was it that touched me?" When no one came forward, Peter said, "Master, the crowds surround you and are pressing in on you!" But knowing it was more than an accidental brush, Jesus said, "Someone touched me, for I perceive that power has gone out from me."

Where Do I Find Healing and Rest?

Realizing she could not hide what had happened, this nameless woman fell down before Him with fear and trembling. Then, in front of the entire crowd, she explained why she had touched Him and gave testimony to her miraculous healing. Afterward, I picture her fear and shame evaporating when she sees the look of love and grace in the eyes of her Savior. Instead of receiving a rebuke for the stolen touch, Jesus tells her to go in peace as her faith has made her well.

Finding Strength in Community

Friend, health challenges can feel humiliating at times—whether we have an issue that others can see, an invisible illness, or an internal mental health struggle. Sometimes, like the woman with the issue of blood, we want to hide in shame. We don't let others in because we fear appearing needy or weak. We want to sneak up behind Jesus and grasp for healing, hoping no one will notice. Yet our heavenly Father calls us to be open about our struggles in a safe Christian community. Oftentimes, during fellowship and prayer among saints, we feel the Savior's touch, thereby encountering the miracle of God's grace together. It took humility for the bleeding woman to experience and share her healing in front of a crowd. Likewise, when we allow others to join in our afflictions, their prayers and affirmations are like Holy Spirit hugs, making *ordinary* things—like a card in the mail on a melancholy day or a meal brought to our doorstep—*extraordinary* means of solace. Rejuvenation of our souls seems to come slowly through day-to-day encouragement and support in a loving body of believers.

Yes, there are times when recovery seems instantaneous, like when the bleeding woman grasped Christ's cloak. But we must remember that this dear woman had already suffered for twelve years. We can't peek into the middle or end of another's story and expect instantaneous results for ourselves. We must remember that God doesn't promise complete physical healing to everyone in this life. Death and disease are part of the curse, and they will receive their final defeat when Christ returns and we experience the new heavens and earth. Friend, God's promise of His presence *through* the waters and rivers of adversity is even better than physical healing because we experience Him in ways we never otherwise would. If the Scriptures say that the Son of Man learned obedience through what He suffered, how much more do we grow in grace and knowledge through our afflictions? Does God bring miraculous physical healing? Absolutely! Does He always and without exception? No. But whatever He does, we can trust it is what is best for us and will bring Him the most glory.

Finding Healing and Rest

My symptoms waxed and waned throughout the years, typical for autoimmune issues. Thirteen years after my symptoms began, I saw an optometrist when I was having ocular problems again. My eyes started their wonky antics during the exam, with drooping eyelids and eyeballs rolling around and losing focus. The young doctor peered into my misfocused pupils and asked if I had ever heard of myasthenia gravis. I responded, "Um, yeah, I was diagnosed with that some years ago in Indiana, but some doctors here in the Atlanta area felt it was a misdiagnosis. I'm no longer receiving treatment for it."

He responded kindly and gently, telling me I needed to find a new neurologist and investigate it again, and he gave me a referral. I got an appointment with a new neurologist reasonably quickly, and thirteen years after the initial prognosis, I was again diagnosed with MG and began treatment.

Since then, finding the best treatment options has been trial and error. Currently, monthly intravenous immunoglobulin (IVIG) infusions have kept me leading a normal (whatever that is!) life. But do I have a life without physical struggles? No. I still have days in bed when I'm having a flare-up, but no longer weeks at a time, as in years past. Often, it's because I've pushed myself too hard, but I experience much improvement with rest.

There is still much mystery surrounding my seizures. I'm still plagued occasionally, but instead of daily occurrences, like years ago, they are infrequent now. Though the doctors say they are unrelated, the convulsions only occur when I'm having an MG flare-up—and typically during a perfect storm of physical and emotional stress and spiritual oppression.

Dear reader, I pray my journey encourages you as you walk through your own valley. May you feel the refreshing shade of Christ's cloak covering your situation. I pray this quote from the daily devotional book *Streams in the Desert*, by L. B. Cowman (1870—1960), encourages you in your bodily afflictions the way it has me:

> The most comforting of David's psalms were pressed out by suffering; and if Paul had not had his thorn in the flesh, we had missed much of that tenderness which quivers in so many of his letters. The present circumstance, which presses so hard against you (if surrendered to Christ), is the best-shaped tool in the Father's hand to chisel you for eternity. Trust Him, then. Do not push away the instrument lest you lose its work.[41]

I must admit I still get discouraged by my physical limitations and autoimmune brain and want to push the shaping instrument away. Yes, I sometimes wish I could accomplish as much as my Christian communicator friends who don't have the same physical limitations. Yet as Mrs. Cowman said in the quote above, our afflictions are "chiseling us for eternity." And when, like Jacob, we stop wrestling with God and begin clinging to Him instead, we feel the tightness and safety of our heavenly Father's grip.

When the unexpected heartbreak of infertility entered my friend Natasha Daniels's life, the shame of being unwanted by her biological father rose to the surface. He had only wanted a boy, and now she couldn't do what girls were created to do. Natasha sought to delight herself in the Lord. Why wasn't God fulling His promise to grant her heart's desire?

> My story is one of grappling with Psalm 37:4: "Delight yourself in the Lord, and He will give you the desires of your heart." Delighting in my family and friends, shopping, crafts, and date nights with my husband were things that came easily for me.
>
> Delighting in the Lord through His Word and prayer likewise brought serenity and joy to my heart. I was doing my part and delighting in Him, but He was not fulfilling my heart's desire for a baby—by quilting one in my womb—and answering my deep longing to become a mommy.
>
> As a little girl, I dreamed of being a wife and a mom. Dreams of marrying my Prince Charming, living in a

cute little cottage with a white picket fence, and having six kids danced in my thoughts. Being a woman who would struggle with infertility never crossed my mind.

My mom and dad had me when they were very young. My dad didn't want me because I was a girl, but I was loved by my mom, grandparents, aunts—and then my stepdad—who came into my life at the age of two. He is my *real* dad.

When I was seventeen, I met my husband and knew he was the one. There was one little problem … he only wanted two kids. But not to worry, I would fix that later. We dated for four years, and on May 15, 1999, we were married.

Slick is an amazing man. He is my best friend, my greatest encourager, and truly loves me like Christ loves the church. I wanted to start a family right away—I couldn't wait to become a mommy. I was so young and naive at the time and just thought we would get pregnant and have our six kids back-to-back. I bought and read every baby book I could find. My husband and I tried to conceive for a year, but month after month, no baby. As I was reading, I came across an article that stated most couples conceive within one year of trying, and if you don't, then you should seek medical advice. I made an appointment to see my gynecologist.

I anticipated the day of my appointment, not knowing what to expect. But I assumed the doctor would provide answers, send me on my way, and I would get pregnant. During the consultation, I expressed my feelings and concerns to my doctor, but since I was only twenty-two and healthy, he assured me that I was young and had plenty of time. He told me not to worry and that it would happen in time. But I was worried and left the clinic feeling defeated and hopeless.

Another year went by and still no success. I sought help from my doctor repeatedly, and his answer was always the same: "You're so young—just relax—it will happen." In the meantime, all my friends were sharing the amazing news that they were expecting. I was happy for them, but I also struggled with jealousy and discontentment. I started to question God, praying and asking: *God, what am I doing wrong? Why won't you give me a baby and fulfill the desire of my heart?*

Insecurity crept in as I thought back to how my biological dad didn't want me because I was a girl, and now I couldn't even do what girls were created to do. Oh, how Satan likes to deceive our minds to believe such lies, to threaten our security and identity as women.

Being a woman of the Word, I remembered reading 1 Corinthians 14:33: "For God is not a God of confusion but of peace." How confusing is that? My journey with infertility left me confused, and peace fled during this struggle. Yet delighting in Jesus is what my life is centered around, and I was faithful in church attendance and served Him by teaching Bible study and leading the children's ministry. Wasn't this proof of my love for Him and my obedience to Psalm 37:4? I was working so hard to delight in Him. Why was He not giving me the desires of my heart?

When God didn't do what I thought He should be doing, I started to doubt His love for me, and I even wondered if God was punishing me for my past sins. I allowed the lies of Satan to consume me, even believing that my husband deserved a wife who could give him a family. My sweet husband didn't feel that way at all. He loved me through it all, and he was so strong and supportive. He comforted me during my grief, and he hurt *for* me. Slick is my rock, and he always knows just what to say and how to make me laugh.

It didn't take long for my jealousy and discontentment to turn into anger and bitterness. I was deeply saddened and even angry when my younger brother, who was still in high school—unmarried and not living for the Lord—announced his girlfriend was pregnant. It just didn't seem fair that they would be rewarded with a baby when they weren't even trying to start a family. Yet here I was, a married woman whose one desire in the whole world was to have babies, and I couldn't conceive. I became resentful toward God more times than I care to admit, and my trust in His promises was on shaky terms.

Yet my soul longed to be comforted by Him, and as I prayed, His presence drew me to continue to read

His Word. Whenever I would open my Bible or read a devotion, it was almost always about adoption—how He adopted us—and how we should care for the widows and the orphans. The Lord was speaking to me through these messages, and I was trying to discern His voice and His will. I began to sense that adoption would somehow become a central part of my life, though I couldn't fathom the details. Reading His Word and focusing on His purpose for our family was healing to my soul, and all the confusion started to vanish. His peace began to invade my heart. As my peace returned, I knew that God wasn't punishing me for anything I had done. Jesus had already taken my punishment for me on the cross, and my heavenly Father loved me deeply.

In March of 2002, I asked my husband if he would be open to looking into adoption if I were not pregnant by the end of the year. He agreed to pray, but he said he wanted me to go to the doctor again. Little did we know that God was already creating our baby in his birth mother's womb.

Fear and excitement took over my thoughts as I waited patiently for the results of some tests the doctor ran. He finally entered the room with the news that I was not ovulating. This revelation sparked hope in my heart, and the doctor prescribed me a low dose of clomiphene to help me ovulate. My husband was praying about adoption, and I was on medication to help me get pregnant. My hope for carrying a child was restored as my doctors didn't mention any concerns regarding infertility.

Yet pregnancy never happened for me, and *infertile* became my label. As one who has now suffered and walked that road, I know it is a very lonely place. Friends and others around me don't understand my pain and don't see infertility as the loss that it is. I grieve what will never be, I grieve the barrenness of my womb, I grieve the action of a sweet baby nursing from my breast, and I grieve the life I had planned for myself. I think of the bleeding woman in the Bible and how deep her disappointment and grief must have been when, year after year, the doctors couldn't heal her.

I remember feeling as if my own soul would bleed out … until one day, I started doing something different. I began delighting in the Lord for who He is, not what He could do for me or give me. When I approached the Lord as a child with open hands, His Word truly became my delight. I was no longer looking for anything more—because I had Jesus, and He was everything. My heavenly Father began to show me that Psalm 37:4 didn't mean he would necessarily give me what I wanted, but He wanted me to have faith in Him and to worship Him while I waited. So I worshipped, and I waited.

You see, I was expecting my motherhood plans to be fulfilled one way, but the Lord wanted to fulfill them in another way. This was when I changed my prayer from, *Lord, please let me become pregnant*—to—*Lord, please let me become a mommy.*

My husband and I are now proud parents to five children through adoption, and what a joy it is to be a mom. Hearing one of our kids call out "Mommy" still brings a smile to my face and fills my soul with gladness. We adopted our first child locally—and while I was taking medicine and praying for conception. The conception did take place, but in his birth mother's womb. Our hearts were overwhelmed with joy the very instant our newborn son was placed in my arms.

We rescued our other four children—two precious little girls and their two older brothers—from a Ukrainian orphanage. Rescue work is dangerous work and sometimes miracles are messy, but we love these children with every fiber of our being. Through the heartache of infertility and the ups and downs of adopting children affected by trauma, God shows us that joy and sorrow can coexist. My cup overflows as He fills it with more of Himself. He is still writing our family story as we delight in Him, and He is giving our souls hope and rest.

Infertility is a huge loss. If this is your story, you may feel alone in this struggle, but you are never alone. Jesus is always with you, and He wants to fulfill your heart's desire. God doesn't promise us a life without pain, but He does promise He will never leave us alone. Grasp the hem of His garment and allow Him to be creative and do it His way. Like the bleeding woman, your heart, too, will find hope and rest.

Wrapped Across God's Shoulders

Those of us with a physical or mental health struggle can worship God while we wait for our multi-faceted and ultimate healing too, whether in this life or the next. Like my friend Natasha, we learn to delight in God for who He is, not in what we want Him to do for us.

With a peaceful heart, we climb up on our heavenly Father's back and, like a gentle shepherd with a lamb, He will wrap us across His shoulders, and we will find rest.

Epilogue

As a pastor's wife and women's ministry leader, I found my identity in the approval of others for many years. However, the endless striving for validation brought me to complete spiritual, physical, and emotional exhaustion.

Friend, have you seen yourself in my journey? You, too, can experience renewal and restoration. The first step is to acknowledge that people-pleasing, insecurity, approval-seeking, responsibility for carrying others' burdens, and fear of rejection are just symptoms. We must recognize that the root cause of those indicators is a disconnect with our perception of God.

In the early years of my marriage, I studied and memorized large portions of the *Westminster Shorter Catechism*—a summary of Christian doctrine through over one hundred questions and answers. I especially love what this catechism says about God in question-and-answer number four: "What is God? God is a Spirit, infinite, eternal, and unchangeable, in His being, wisdom, power, holiness, justice, goodness, and truth."[42] Those lovely attributes and descriptions of the great I Am are magnificent and true. Therefore, we should indeed worship God in His holiness, with reverential awe, and respect His justice and righteousness.

Yet Scripture teaches us that God is also a loving and tender father and shepherd to those who have received His Son as their

Lord and Savior—a concept I didn't fully grasp until several years ago. Pastor Ray Ortlund of Renewal Ministries talks of the New Testament's emphasis on God as Father:

> Though God remains holy and majestic in our eyes, Jesus adds a strikingly clear emphasis on God as Father—both his Father and our Father (John 20:17). It is Jesus who calls God "Abba, Father" (Mark 14:36). It is Jesus who teaches us to pray to God as our Father (Matthew 6:9). It is the Spirit of the Son who leads us into intimacy with God as our own Abba Father (Galatians 4:6). Now we know that, as our Father, God cares for us and provides for us (Matthew 6:25–34). As our Father, he hears and answers our prayers (Matthew 7:7–11). As our Father, he disciplines us (Hebrews 12:3–11). As our Father, he receives us and forgives us and rejoices over us when in repentance we come home to him (Luke 15:11–32). That God the Father has made himself God our Father means that he is personally, emotionally, and even sacrificially involved with us.[43]

Ortlund gives us a lovely picture of Christ Jesus's description of God as His Father and as our Father—and God's tender affection for His Son and for us. Ortlund also references Luke 15 as a display of God's personal and emotional involvement in the lives of His people—a Father who runs to meet the prodigal as he returns home after forsaking the emptiness of the world.

Where Do I Find Healing and Rest?

Dear reader, as we begin to grasp who God is as our heavenly Father and start living as His blood-bought sons and daughters:

- Like Moses, we release our fear of failure and confidently walk in the good works God has already provided for us.
- Like Abigail, we will speak the truth, exercise godly wisdom, discover the boldness to leave abusive relationships, and learn the importance of healthy boundaries.
- Like the sinful woman, we will experience freedom from the fear of rejection and find our place at the feet of Jesus.
- Like the woman at the well, we will release our shame and run and tell others about our approval in Christ.
- Like Mary Magdalene, we will find renewed strength and purpose and rediscover the joy lacking in our work and ministry.
- Like Martha, we will release the endless striving for security and validation through approval-seeking and find rest in Christ's finished work.
- Like the woman with an issue of blood, we will release our fear of other people's opinions and rest in our heavenly Father's complete affirmation of us.

Friend, I would love to hear how you have experienced significance and security in your heavenly Father's embrace. I also have limited lay counseling appointments if you are looking for a one-on-one emotional healing coach. Or I would love the privilege of serving your women's group as a keynote or retreat speaker.

Your securely held sister,

Cheryl

For more information, I can be reached at: CherylLutz.com

A Prayer for His Beloved

Dear heavenly Father, I praise You again for the privilege of coming before Your throne through the blood of Your beloved Son. Please help me serve You and others from a place of rest—in the finished work of the Lord Jesus Christ. Father, help me release the fear of failure and confidently walk in the good works You have already provided for me, giving me the ability to release the endless striving for security and validation. Please help me release my fear of rejection and find my place at the feet of Jesus. Please help me release my shame and run and tell others about my approval in Christ. Please help me release my fear of other people's opinions and rest in Your complete affirmation of me. In Jesus's name, amen.

A Note from Cheryl's Husband

King David, the man after God's own heart, wrote in his epic Psalm 119:71, "It is good for me that I have been afflicted; that I might learn thy statutes." That is an amazing confession! Study David's life, and you will better know why. Even more remarkable is what Paul wrote concerning David's Lord: "Though He was a Son, *yet* He learned obedience by the things which He suffered" (Hebrews 5:8 NKJV). Christ Jesus, our only and all-sufficient Savior, proved His perfect obedience and submission to the Father's will by treading the *Via Dolorosa* throughout the entirety of His life. The culmination of His suffering was on the cross. David learned more of the depths of God's Word through his afflictions, and Christ learned perfect obedience through His sufferings—and thus became "the author of eternal salvation" (Hebrews 5:9).

I am filled with gratitude that my beloved wife of thirty-four years was moved by God to document her afflictions. As we faced these challenges together, we gained valuable insight from them. While I would not have included such struggles if I were the one writing the story of our lives, we are thankful that we were able to grow in our faith together in the face of these hardships.

We have come to understand more about the truth of God's Word and the glory of Immanuel's grace, which has persevered us through every circumstance and season of life together. As a young couple, we vowed to one another the day we were married:

> I, Alan/Cheryl, take thee, Cheryl/Alan, to be my
> wedded wife/husband;
> And I do promise and covenant
> Before God and these witnesses,
> To be thy loving and faithful husband/wife,
> In plenty and in want,
> In joy and in sorrow,
> In sickness and in health,
> As long as we both shall live.

My dear wife loves rollercoasters and the wild rides they give, but it's only natural to hope that your life experiences don't have such steep climbs and perilous falls.

I asked to write a few paragraphs in order to affirm the reality of the physical, emotional, and spiritual struggles Cheryl faced growing up and during our child-raising years. I am proud of her willingness to be transparently honest in hopes of helping others navigate their storms, deserts, discouragements, and dead ends. She faithfully studies and teaches the Holy Scriptures and is true to the Spirit of Christ Jesus in her testimony and counsel. What an amazing person to have as my life's best friend! I better understand the reality of being securely held in God's embrace, thanks to her. She wrote on her Valentine's Day card to me this year: "I love you! And I am enjoying these quieter days to just be together." Amen! And by God's grace, we will continue our journey as one in Him.

—Alan Lutz

About the Author

Cheryl Lutz is an inspirational speaker, certified lay counselor, Bible teacher, retired pastor's wife, and recovering people-pleaser! Her passion is in helping women break the power of other people's opinions and rest securely in God's embrace.

Through her blog, newsletter, books, and speaking engagements, Cheryl guides women to discover their true identity as God's daughters and walk confidently in the good works He has created for them. With a focus on biblical truth and personal stories, her mission is to equip women to overcome insecurity and live as God's masterpiece, radiating the beauty of their Creator.

Cheryl and her husband, Alan, live in a quaint cabin snuggled in the North Georgia Mountains, a good gift from their Abba Father. They have four adult children and a bonus son by marriage. Cheryl is a proud Mimi to Elle, Luna, and Yoda, their two granddogs and grandcat!

Please reach out to Cheryl on her website and let her know how she can serve your women's group! CherylLutz.com

Notes

Chapter 1

1. Jo Ann Fore, *When a Woman Finds Her Voice: Overcoming Life's Hurts & Using Your Story to Make a Difference* (Texas: Leafwood Publishers), 1.

2. "John Calvin's Bible Commentary, Hebrews 11:23," BibliaPlus Online, https://www.bibliaplus.org/en/commentaries/3/john-calvins-bible-commentary/hebrews/11/23.

3. "I Am Who I Am," resource by John Piper, Desiring God, https://www.desiringgod.org/messages/i-am-who-i-am.

Chapter 2

4. Charles Haddon Spurgeon, "A Vile Weed and a Fair Flower," Spurgeon's Sermons (V24), (1878), https://ccel.org/ccel/spurgeon/sermons24/sermons24.lix.html.

Chapter 3

5. Rosaria Butterfield, "Can a Practicing Homosexual be a Practicing Christian?" Rosaria Butterfield (blog), February 14, 2018, https://rosariabutterfield.com/new-blog/2018/2/14/can-a-practicing-homosexual-be-a-practicing-christian.

6. Charles Haddon Spurgeon, "The Woman Which was a Sinner," The Spurgeon Center for Biblical Preaching at Midwestern

Seminary, March 22, 1868, https://www.spurgeon.org/resource-library/sermons/the-woman-which-was-a-sinner/#flipbook/.

Chapter 4
7. C. S. Lewis, *The Screwtape Letters* (New York: Harper Collins, 1996), ix.
8. Ruth Graham, *Forgiving My Father, Forgiving Myself: An Invitation to the Miracle of Forgiveness* (Michigan: Baker Books), 37.
9. Graham, 154.
10. Charles Haddon Spurgeon, "Mary Magdalene," The Spurgeon Center for Biblical Preaching at Midwestern Seminary, https://www.spurgeon.org/resource-library/sermons/mary-magdalene/#flipbook/.
11. C. L. Chase, *Good, Good Father: Knowing God as He Wants to Be Known:* (Scotland, UK: Christian Focus Publications, e-book conversion by Vivlia Limited), 40.
12. Graham, 171.

Chapter 5
13. Google Online Dictionary, definitions from Oxford Languages, *Definition of Shame*, https://www.google.com/search?client=safari&rls=en&q=shame&ie=UTF-8&oe=UTF-8.
14. *Christianity Today*, July/August 2002, Christian History, *John Newton, Reformed Slave Trader,* https://www.christianitytoday.com/history/people/pastorsandpreachers/john-newton.html.
15. Google Online Dictionary, definitions from Oxford Languages, *Definition of Wretch*, https://www.google.com/search?client=safari&rls=en&q=wretch&ie=UTF-8&oe=UTF-8.
16. Bible Dictionaries, *Holman Bible Dictionary*, StudyLight.org, *Conviction,* https://www.studylight.org/dictionaries/eng/hbd/c/conviction.html.

17. Kegan Mosier, "What Am I Feeling? Shame or Conviction," *Cornerstone Christian Counseling* (online article), September 17, 2015, https://christiancounselingco.com/what-am-i-feeling-shame-or-conviction/.

Chapter 6

18. Debbie McDaniel, "Who was Elisabeth Elliot?," Crosswalk.com (online article), June 17, 2015, https://www.crosswalk.com/faith/spiritual-life/inspiring-quotes/40-inspiring-quotes-from-elisabeth-elliot.html.

19. Charles Haddon Spurgeon, "Hagar at the Fountain," The Spurgeon Center for Biblical Preaching at Midwestern Seminary, https://www.spurgeon.org/resource-library/sermons/hagar-at-the-fountain/#flipbook/.

20. Jade Mazarin, "God Is Working in Your Waiting," Desiring God, February 20, 2017, https://www.desiringgod.org/articles/god-is-working-in-your-waiting.

21. McDaniel.

22. Spurgeon, "Hagar."

Chapter 7

23. Captain Anie Trimmer, "Jochebed: A Courageous and Astute Mother," The Salvation Army, Women's Ministries, USA Territory, https://usw-womensministries.org/jochebed-a-courageous-and-astute-mother/.

24. Christine Trimpe, *Seeking Joy Through the Gospel of Luke: A Christmas to Calvary Advent Countdown,* (Washington: Redemption Press), Cover Copy.

Chapter 8

25. John Newton, "Amazing Grace," https://www.hymnal.net/en/hymn/h/313.

26. Samuel John Stone, "The Church's One Foundation," https://hymnary.org/text/the_churchs_one_foundation.

Chapter 9

27. Marshall Segal, "You Cannot Please God and People, Five Remedies for the Fear of Man," Desiring God, March 15, 2021, https://www.desiringgod.org/articles/you-cannot-please-god-and-people.

28. Ibid.

29. Shelly Miller, *Rhythms of Rest: Finding the Spirit of Sabbath in a Busy World* (Minnesota: Bethany House Publishers), 102.

30. Billy Graham Evangelistic Association, Answers By BGEA, "What Does It Mean to Bear One Another's Burdens?," November 17, 2020, https://billygraham.org/answer/what-does-it-mean-to-bear-one-anothers-burdens/.

31. Joni Eareckson Tada, *The God I Love, A Lifetime of Walking with Jesus* (Grand Rapids, MI: Zondervan, 2003), 218.

Chapter 10

32. "Mary Had a Little Lamb," Poetry Foundation, https://www.poetryfoundation.org/poems/46954/mary-had-a-little-lamb.

33. Jon Bloom, "Why Jethro? The Wisdom of What God Doesn't Say," Desiring God, October 5, 2012, https://www.desiringgod.org/articles/why-jethro-the-wisdom-of-what-god-doesnt-say.

34. Alexander Maclaren, "The Warrior Peace," Christian Classics Ethereal Library, accessed June 9, 2023,

https://ccel.org/ccel/maclaren/iicor_tim/iicor_tim.
iii.i.v.html?queryID=25848837&resultID=143569.
35. Mary Anna Jackson, *Life and Letters of General Thomas J. Jackson: Letters from Stonewall Jackson during the American Civil War* (Harper & Brothers, 1892, 2019), 3297.

Chapter 11

36. Jon Bloom, "Whom Are You Really Serving?," Desiring God, March 23, 2012, https://www.desiringgod.org/articles/whom-are-you-really-serving.
37. Ibid.
38. Ibid.
39. Johann Heinrich Schroder, "One Thing's Needful," https://hymnary.org/text/one_things_needful_lord_this_treasure.

Chapter 12

40. Sue Poorman Richards and Larry Richards, *Every Woman in the Bible*, (Nashville, TN: T. Nelson Publishers, 1999), 189.
41. L. B. Cowman, "Streams in the Desert," Crosswalk.com, July 19, 2022, https://www.crosswalk.com/devotionals/desert/streams-in-the-desert-july-19th.html.

Epilogue

42. Christian Classics Ethereal Library, Westminster Shorter Catechism (1647), https://www.ccel.org/creeds/westminster-shorter-cat.html.
43. Ray Ortlund, "What Does the Bible Say About God as Our Father?," Crossway, June 19, 2022, https://www.crossway.org/articles/what-does-the-bible-say-about-god-as-our-father/.

Recommended Resources for Responding to Abuse

(Resources from the website of Diane Langberg, PhD, DianeLangberg.com)

Books

- **A Church Called Tov: Forming a Goodness Culture that Resists Abuses of Power and Promotes Healing,** Scot McKnight, Laura Barringer (Tyndale, 2020).
- **Something's Not Right: Decoding the Hidden Tactics of Abuse and Freeing Yourself from Its Power,** Wade Mullen (Tyndale, 2020).
- **When Dad Hurts Mom: Helping Your Children Heal the Wounds of Abuse,** Lundy Bancroft (Berkley, 2005).
- **Why Does He DO That?: Inside the Minds of Angry and Controlling Men,** Lundy Bancroft (Berkley, 2003).
- **A Cry for Justice: How the Evil of Domestic Abuse Hides in Your Church!,** Jeff Crippen (Calvary Press, 2012).
- **Unholy Charade: Unmasking the Domestic Abuser in the Church,** Jeff Crippen (Justice Keepers Publishing, 2015)
- **Trauma and Recovery: The Aftermath of Violence— From Domestic Abuse to Political Terror,** Judith Herman (Basic Books, 1997).

- **Counseling Survivors of Sexual Abuse,** Diane Langberg (Xulon Press, 2003).
- **On the Threshold of Hope: Opening the Door to Hope and Healing for Survivors of Sexual Abuse,** Diane Langberg (Tyndale House Publishing, 1999).
- **On the Threshold of Hope Workbook,** Diane Langberg (Xulon Press, 2014).
- **The Spiritual Impact of Sexual Abuse (mini book),** Diane Langberg (New Growth Press, 2017).
- **Suffering and the Heart of God: How Trauma Destroys and Christ Restores,** Diane Langberg (New Growth Press, 2015).
- **Naming Our Abuse: God's Pathway to Healing for Male Sexual Abuse Survivors,** Andrew Schmutzer (Kregel Publications, 2016).
- **Your Wife Was Sexually Abused,** John Courtright and Sid Rogers (Zondervan, 1994).
- **The Long Journey Home: Understanding and Ministering to the Sexually Abused,** Andrew Schmutzer (Wipf and Stock Publishers, 2011).
- **No Visible Bruises: What We Don't Know About Domestic Violence Can Kill Us,** Rachel Louise Snyder (Bloomsbury Publishing, 2019).
- **Domestic Abuse: Recognize, Respond, Rescue,** Darby Strickland (P&R Publishing, 2018).
- **Black and White Bible, Black and Blue Wife: My Story of Finding Hope after Domestic Abuse,** Ruth Tucker (Zondervan, 2016).

- **Emotionally Destructive Marriage: How to Find Your Voice and Reclaim Your Hope,** Leslie Vernick (WaterBrook, 2013).

Websites

- **www.netgrace.org—G.R.A.C.E. (Godly Response to Abuse in a Christian Environment).**
- www.lundybancroft.com—Lundy Bancroft: Workshop **leader and consultant on domestic abuse and child maltreatment.**
- **www.annasalter.com—Dr. Anna Salter: Training, consultant, and publications on sexual abuse.**

Bibliography of Books and Websites for Story Contributors

Brown, Melony, *Challenges Won't Stop Me: An Interactive Survival Guide for Overcoming & Thriving*, (Georgia: Fiction House Press), https://melonybrown.com.

Brown, Shelly, https://www.facebook.com/shellybrown68.

Daniels, Natasha, https://www.natashalynndaniels.com.

England, Christina, https://www.christinaengland.com/#page.

Eversole, Missy, *Transformed, Not Conformed: Embracing a Life-Changing Approach to Spiritual Habits* (Washington: Redemption Press), https://missyeversole.com.

Lafler, J. C., *Love—What's God Got to Do with It?* (Washington: Redemption Press), https://jclafler.com.

Linkletter, Missy, www.missylinkletter.com.

Mantelli, Phylis, *Unmothered: Life with a Mom Who Couldn't Love Me* (Washington: Redemption Press), https://www.phylismantelli.com.

Ruddell, Michelle, *Welcome to the Club—I'm Sorry You're Here: Hope for Grieving Parents* (Independently Published), https://michelleruddell.com.

Trimpe, Christine, *Seeking Joy Through the Gospel of Luke: A Christmas to Calvary Advent Countdown* (Washington: Redemption Press), https://christinetrimpe.com.

ORDER INFORMATION

To order additional copies of this book, please visit
www.redemption-press.com.
Also available at Christian bookstores, Amazon, and Barnes and Noble.

Printed in the USA
CPSIA information can be obtained
at www.ICGtesting.com
JSHW020220301123
52751JS00003B/34